Living Solo

Living Solo

Adrienne Salinger

Andrews McMeel
Publishing

Kansas City

www.andrewsmcmeel.com

98 99 00 01 02 TWP 10 9 8 7 6 5 4 3 2 1

Library of Congress Cataloging-in-Publication Data
Living solo / [edited by] Adrienne Salinger.
p. cm.
ISBN: 0-8362-6753-2 (pbk.)
1. Single persons—United States—Interviews. 2. Single persons—United States—Portraits. 3. Living alone—United States. 4. Portrait photography—United States.
5. Salinger, Adrienne. I. Salinger, Adrienne.
HQ800.4.U6I58 1998
301'.01—dc21
98-14365
CIP

ATTENTION: SCHOOLS AND BUSINESSES

Andrews McMeel books are available at quantity discounts with bulk purchase for educational, business, or sales promotional use. For information, please write to: Special Sales Department, Andrews McMeel Publishing, 4520 Main Street, Kansas City, Missouri 64111.

For their endless encouragement, intelligence, and humor, this book is for my parents, Linda K. and Herb Smith

Contents

Acknowledgments

Thanks to Vincent Borrelli, the MacDowell Colony, the Puffin Foundation, LightWork, Paul Alan Smith, Jim Colbert, and my editor, Rick Hill. I'm very grateful to all the people who let me into their lives and made this book possible.

Introduction

I don't remember when I first noticed that I live alone. Really alone. Maybe it was when I bought my first house by myself. Or maybe it was when I noticed that it had been about three months since I had used a plate, preferring instead the decadence of eating "takeout" over the sink while talking on the phone.

When I was growing up, I loved the stories of ten-year-old Pippi Longstocking, who lived alone without parents or rules in an enormous dilapidated house. She baked cookies the size of her kitchen floor and ate them all day long. When I was eight, I reread often a story about a boy who left the suburbs and moved to a mountain to subsist by himself inside the trunk of a tree. With his trained falcon on his shoulder, he foraged for berries. Although these images of living alone remembered from my childhood have been eclipsed by the more complex realities of my adult experiences, somewhere, deep down, I recognize the relative joy of controlling my own space and marking my own time.

The most recent census report documents that there are more than twenty-five million of us living alone in this country. We have nothing in common. We have everything in common. We live in big cities and small towns. We eat over the sink and in bed—and sometimes at a table. We find things where we left them. We always know where the good scissors are. We own the remote control. We are the people who sometimes celebrate holidays alone. We sing out loud when we play CDs. We talk to our pets. We are sometimes lonely. We are often successful and driven. We are sometimes poor and trapped. We have good friends. We have lovers. We are old. We are young. We are gay and straight. We are divorced, widowed, single, living on opposite coasts from our partners.

Possibly this is the first generation in which living alone is presumed to be a legitimate choice rather than a declaration of defeat; unprecedented numbers of people now choose to keep their own homes, to decorate them, and to entertain in them without overt societal pressure to adapt to specific notions of family living. Advertisers are finally courting us to eat frozen single meals, sleep alone in luxury, buy cars, take vacations, shop for insurance, rent videos. And yet this enormous group remains invisible. Until recently, living "alone" was considered an aberration, a transient state within which individuals were identified by the culture as submissively awaiting mates in order to fully participate in society. People existed in a state of suspension and were eager to become part of a "couple," a blissful union in which major purchases and life decisions would be compromises of taste and desire. However, in the course of writing this book I learned that living alone isn't about being "single." Most of the people I photographed are involved in relationships. Many are committed to long-term partnerships yet maintain separate residences.

People live alone for many reasons—some by choice, some by circumstance, some temporarily, and some forever. As someone who lives alone now, but hasn't always, I feel able to understand some of the complications. Without other people to help govern the events of daily living or judge the "normalcy" of particular habits, a certain eccentricity is allowed to emerge. Eccentricity can be a good thing. It can make us unique, creative, unusual, mysterious, and sometimes idiosyncratic.

This book is about how people define themselves in their spaces when they don't have to compromise. The photographs and texts show the diversity and courage of the individual life. Our living spaces reveal a lot about us. What we own and display is often at odds with our public identity. Environments emerge that celebrate the tastes, hobbies, and impulses of the individual—environments that, if the spaces were shared, might otherwise be relegated to the basement. There is no stereotype. I met a man who collects Tiffany lamps with the proceeds he earned from his role as Mr. Clean. I met a woman whose father was a Japanese country-western singer—specializing in Hank Williams. She's just released her first CD in Chicago. I met a man who exercises by walking back and forth in his house—160 round trips makes four miles.

I use a 4 x 5 view camera, strobe equipment, and video to capture the audio without losing the body language and nuance. I traveled around the country for six months, from California to New York, photographing and interviewing. I met people from twenty-two to ninety-one years old, in Laundromats, waiting in line for a clothing sale in a snowstorm, in bookstores, on the street. I asked them if I could come home with them and spend the day. And invariably they said, "Why not?"

While reading the texts that accompany the photographs, one may wonder why some people chose to articulate the more difficult times of their lives rather than the high points. As humans, too often we don't analyze our good days. I've never met anyone who wakes up happy and spends much time trying to figure out what events in their childhood or environment have led them to feel that way. They simply feel happy. Yet when we feel sad, or even introspective, we spend hours painstakingly examining the malaise.

When we look at a photograph, we make certain assumptions. We assume that the photograph is a fact, that it has veracity. This is not true. These images are constructed—as are all images. I don't pretend objectivity. My presence is in all of these images. I use the tools of photography: framing, lighting, camera choice, film, pose. I make decisions that perhaps tell more about how I feel, who I am, than about someone else. The memories and stories people tell me and the ways I edit them may be at odds with how the participants view themselves. I am not a journalist. I am not a sociologist. I am an artist with an intense curiosity about—and respect for—the individual life.

This book depicts a truth about people who live alone, a truth defined by a particular moment. The photographs are not altered in any way, and the words are directly from the people's mouths. But if there is a problem, it is that I controlled the camera to make the image I thought was the significant one. And I selected out of the hours of transcribed conversations that sliver I judged to be important or representative. So we see that the truth I'm depicting is filtered through my senses and must necessarily be partly my own.

Living Solo

Abby Bayouth

I was married during the war because it was the spirit of the times to get married. The boys wanted to have somebody to leave behind and all that stuff. I married somebody who was very nice. I hardly knew him, but I thought he was very sophisticated because he had gone to school at the American University in Beirut. We went to Fort Wayne for two months, and then he was shipped overseas for two years.

Our house was a haven for war brides. We used to sit around the dining room table and write letters to our loves. We had no idea of what the war was really like. We'd go to the movies and see the newsreels of these poor boys being blown to bits. And we'd say, Oh dear, I hope they're not ours. We had no concept of the stupidity of war.

I stayed married twenty-seven years, but I wanted out a lot earlier. I wanted to love him. He couldn't help his background any more than I could help mine. I went to four lawyers before I could get divorced. It's so sordid. Of course he was a decent person, you know. He didn't drink, he wasn't abusive—except emotionally.

People thought it was a very happy home because we had a very beautiful house.

I started an interior decorating business. I did have some fabulous clients. I'm not a practical person, I'm afraid. If I went to a showroom, I'd buy every sample in sight—but I didn't waste anything. Practicality doesn't bring adventure at all.

I rent this place, but I made it into a home regardless. Somebody will say that's extravagant. Well, I invest in living. It's a good rental. They're very good to me because they know I take care of it. I put in my garden. I covered the terrace. I walled it in.

When I have money, I spend it. When I don't, I get along. In the end, what difference does it all make? I certainly don't envy anybody. If I ever envied anything, it was a happy marriage. And now I don't even envy that.

Alan Metzger

I had always been interested in sex. I came to Los Angeles after I got divorced and I spent about six months staring at the ocean. Thinking about life. I've got three kids and a job which is very interesting to me. But sex is a really important part of my life. I'm lucky because I'm a director, so I can act out my fantasies and try to express myself through the jobs I get.

Everything to me is sexual in nature. Sex is the great driving force of one's life. This place has a sexual component to it. I'm speaking about rooms and so on. Sex has a million different, billion different facets. I find sex is a subject most people want to talk about. Everybody has experience about it and everyone's interested in talking about it. How do power and sex fit in? To me, those are questions that are interesting as hell.

I like to have intimate knowledge of people. I like people to reveal themselves to me. The human thing is all about sexual energy. But I don't fuck a lot of women at the same time.

I've got some friends who are gay. And I think there's a certain sexuality in the relationship. It never goes anywhere. It's nothing physical, but I would say that it's not something that I feel threatened by, and it's something that I enjoy.

Love and passion are something that to men is kind of like a loss of face, loss of control. Men are really dopes about it. Most men are scared of women because women are smarter than men in the man-woman arena. Men don't like to admit weakness. I'm crazy about women. I'm crazy about women. They got a really great thing going. Plus they make me laugh. I like to watch them. I like to touch them.

I would say most people don't like sex. It's surprised me a lot to have dates with women and they're a certain way—and then you get to the fucking stage, and they're a different way. Much more inhibited in the fucking process. Or more nervous. I think that the whole sex thing is something that, to do it well, you have to be pretty open.

You have to really open yourself to the other person. Literally. And that's a scary process for most people.

Albert Fanning

My friends will tell you that I'm not very revealing. I avoid talking about myself. Everybody has two faces. I try real hard just to have one face.

There are five kids in our family. I'm the fourth. I don't speak to my family, though, and my family doesn't speak to me. There was a dispute after my mother's death. They think I ripped off her estate and I mishandled things. I had power of attorney. I did some things that I had discussed with *her*, and the family was never really interested in getting the full story. I took care of her for a little over a year while she was dying of cancer. They never really understood the debt I went into to do that. It's their problem, not mine. I sleep fine. It hurts a lot, for sure, and it's lonely. While my mother was ill, I kept in touch with every one of them each week, gave them updates, reports, told them when she only had a short time left and that they should all come home when she was about to die. They all did. My mom was a great lady. She was a terrific lady.

Oh, your smile is so beautiful, they used to say. I didn't like being attractive to women because it always seemed to me that women liked me for the way I looked and not for the way I was. And that's always bothered me. So I tend not to trust women when they're attracted to me. I know this is going to sound like I'm boasting, but I'm not: women fall in love with me. Easily and a lot. Over the years, that's scared me.

You patronize yourself immediately when you come back from Vietnam by saying when you were there you did good things. You have to do that to maintain your sanity. And we did do good things. You have to start saying it right away. While I was there, I did good things. I didn't just kill people, and I didn't just blow up things. I did good things, too. I didn't call them gooks. I didn't call them slant-eyes. I didn't treat them as inferior to me.

Fifteen years I was home from Vietnam, and I bought a couple acres out in the country and it was near a game preserve and I hadn't been there too long and all of a sudden two armored helicopters came flying over my place and before I realized what was happening, I was in a corner shaking. Just the rattling sound. I was going crazy. And I didn't know why. I had no idea that it was from the sound of the helicopters. That sound means you're coming from the jungle or going back to the jungle. And you're gonna get shot at and you're going to shoot and it's crazy.

You should have had the choice. If you don't want to fight for the country, for someone else's ideals, or someone else's idea of how another country should be run, then you should have had that right.

Amy Brakarsh

I've enjoyed decorating this house. I took most of the chances in here with the colors. I wanted a color that would be warm, a color I could wrap around myself. You put the little paint chips on the wall, and then you invite fifteen people over and say, What do you think? and everyone picks a different chip. Then you make up your own mind. And they never look the way they do in the chips. I've made mistakes. I have other colors in the house that I can't wait to paint over. It's sort of hit-and-miss. There's no science to it. Nothing is unchangeable.

I go back and forth about living alone. Sometimes it feels lonely. Sometimes I feel like it would be nice to come home and have someone to talk to. Home is my hideaway quiet place where I get things done for myself. And it's almost like this is my personal world here and the outside world is my public world. And so I find I'm always pushing myself to go out and do things because that's where my social life is.

I'd like to get married. I'd like to be in a relationship. I'd like to have someone to share things with. I think that's something I definitely lack. I'm not all that attracted to babies, but I like the sense of family. I have two older brothers, and that's very important to me. I like the whole idea of my family getting together, even though we all bitch and moan and have our problems with each other. I like the community of it.

Sometimes when I look at my parents—they're getting old—and I feel like I have to start doing it for myself. It's all been done for me up until now. It's sort of at a point where I feel like I have to start taking action.

I remember when I started to feel like women were *the way*. My parents and a couple of their friends who had kids used to rent a couple different houses on the Cape in the summers. The men would work all week and come up on the weekends.

I have these really clear memories of being on the verandas with these beautiful women. My mother is just gorgeous. They were all really in their prime. Beautiful women with huge personalities.

I used to just sit and watch these women with their beautiful legs and their red toenail polish sit around and smoke and drink cocktails at eleven, flip through glamour magazines. These gorgeous, gorgeous women who were totally self-sufficient and really didn't need men in their lives.

On the weekends, all of the fathers would come. And all of the fathers really thought they were in control. And the women had like this unspoken conspiracy going on. They lived this totally free and joyous life, and as soon as Friday around dusk came, everything changed because the men were coming, so they switched back into this other thing.

They let the men walk ahead of them. They would walk three feet behind and chat together and fix dinner, and fix the drinks, and be polite and go to the cocktail parties.

And the men thought the women were there waiting for them devotedly. And then Sunday night would come around, and the men would leave, and then it was like a big celebration again.

And so I always felt like the men were pathetic. Because they never understood what the women were really like. That the women were such different animals than they were.

That's when I realized that women were just awesome creatures that need to be appreciated in every possible way.

Anne Meredith

Barbara Blanks

I was sitting on the couch one night—I swear this was all it was—and my husband was grading papers and I just said to myself, I'm really tired of being what everybody wants me to be. I want freedom to be me. And when I went to bed that night, something changed, because when I woke up the next morning, the ball was already moving. I was never the same again.

One of the things I was saying when the lid blew off is there really was *no* God as the church defined it. This was out of the blue. I didn't talk to anybody. I was from a rural background in West Tennessee, and for many years I was in church morning, noon, and night. I said to my husband—of course, you could imagine: here was this man who had actually done some preaching as part of his background, and I had sung in the choir—and I was saying that I didn't believe in God anymore. That God was in us! And in a sense *we* were God. Oh Lord, was that not well-received!

I wanted to burn down all the churches. I wanted everybody to have the freedom to get to their own soul. I felt like the church was very directive and controlling.

It was a journey I absolutely had to do. I bottomed out by choice. I had a lot of the same characteristics that I read later apply to people who are having nervous breakdowns. Only I knew I wasn't having a nervous breakdown.

I did a lot of reading. The only way I could survive was to look for a place where I felt I belonged, and that was the Chapel Hill university library. So I read some existentialists. I managed to survive and I learned a lot of things that I needed to learn and gradually the pieces came together again, little by little by little.

That spirit that lives within us controls this culture. And it will control any culture forever and a day. People can either learn about it and respect it or live with the consequences. It can get worse.

I didn't really want the divorce, but I was getting very tired of the junk that was going on in the marriage. I felt like there had to be some better way for me to live. I had been brought up like a lot of other people my age: stick it out—that's what my mother did. I'm fifty-seven. It wore her out, it really did.

The longer I stay here, the stronger I get, and the stronger I get, the less I want somebody in the house with me all the time. I don't want to be cooking anybody's meals. I don't want to be washing anybody's clothes. I don't want to be vacuuming behind anybody but me.

I liked to play with dolls. I played with girls. I didn't like sports. I was basically a textbook case. I loved art. I loved pretty things. I enjoyed dressing up in my mother's clothes when I was little, although I've never been into drag as an adult. I remember once being at my grandmother's house when I was little, and she had this low bureau with all her jewelry. And I remember these crescent-shaped earrings—costume jewelry. I thought they were sapphires and diamonds and rubies. I put them on and I remember going, Aren't I *pretty*? and just looking and seeing my parents horrified. I don't remember them chastising me, but I remember seeing the Look, and I knew something was wrong with this, but I didn't know what it was. So I learned to hide it. I would go to my friend Laura's house and we would play Barbies, but I'd make her lock the door 'cause I didn't want anybody to find out. It was a big secret, and I loved it.

One of my favorite memories of Fernando and me was when we came back from the doctor after he had his T cells checked. He didn't want me to go to the doctor with him. But I said, I'm not going to leave you. I want to be with you for this. He was HIV-positive for eleven years. No sickness.

My favorite Barbie was one that Laura had. It was Prom Night Barbie. From 1963 or something. I almost screamed because I found it in a store. The manufacturer had done a thirtieth anniversary reissue, and it brought back all these memories of how much I loved it when I was a child. They had issued the anniversary edition of Solo in the Spotlight that Fernando loved. I got it for him. He was in heaven. We played Barbies all that night.

I was so in love. I adored him. He said on one of the first nights, "Billy, we shine in very similar colors." And we did. And we made each other shine more brightly. I was willing to sit by his bed while he twisted up and became diseased and sick. Anything. I would have stayed with him.

It was a very busy week for me at work because we were taping an episode that I had written. We taped my show on Thursday, and Friday morning I went into work. Everybody was *full* of congratulations. Oh, what a wonderful show it was. It was the first good show of the season. And it was a gay wedding episode. It was sort of a groundbreaking kind of episode, and it had been extremely well received. Professionally, it was a real high point. And I was in a room and someone came in and said I had a phone call and I immediately knew what had happened. And I rushed back to my office and the woman on the phone said, "Fernando is dead. He killed himself." And I just started to sob.

Bill Walker

Bruce Lederman

I haven't spoken to my mother in a couple of years. Partly because of telling her I'm gay, and partly because of other issues. In some ways it's hard, and in some ways it isn't. You get used to not speaking with a person. You try to imagine what it will be like when one day you will not be able to—either because you won't be here or she won't be here. She left a very bitter message on my answering machine. It was extraordinarily crass. Probably she views my being gay as a rejection of her. She took it very personally. Being gay has nothing to do with her, which in a way would probably upset her also.

It's a shame, but there are a lot of things that are shameful. My father and I, we have a nice relationship.

I've lived alone since senior year of college. I enjoy it. For a while there, after law school, I didn't have many friends, so I'd spend a lot of time in the apartment. I would go for a weekend without speaking to anyone. I wasn't lonely. I could always talk to people on the phone.

I had a lot of straight friends, and they started dating more seriously and getting married. And I knew what was taking place; I knew I was still hanging out with them. I wasn't progressing on my parallel track, I was just hitching a ride on their freight car. I knew that it wouldn't work forever, but I was comfortable with it. And so were they. And that was fine. After law school, they started moving out to the suburbs, people started to begin their families, and I wasn't really confident enough in myself to start making those decisions that would get me on *my* track.

I'm never here. As a matter of fact, if you took out the amount of time that I sleep here, I spend more time in the health club than I spend in this apartment. I work out four or five times a week. I lift weights and I'll do some cardiovascular. I wanted to sort of change my body type. I wanted to look different, so I started lifting weights and gained thirty pounds and that was kind of fun. That was over the course of about five years.

I follow Jewish law as much as I can because by doing so I re-create creation in my own life. I create order. I keep kosher. That means I follow a set of dietary laws, most of which involve the separation of life and death. The separation of dairy and meat. Life is represented by the milk, and meat itself is from the carcass—death. Keeping kosher is a political act. If you're dealing with a community that's in exile and has no home, how do you maintain an identity when you are living in a diaspora? One way to do that is to have dietary laws, which in a very basic way prevent you from intermingling with the neighbors. Think about it. You can't go down and break bread with someone who isn't following the same dietary laws as you. You can go to their home, but then you can't participate in the meal. So it is certainly a way of creating identity.

Byron Vreeland

I was walking out to lunch one day and there was an agent who was undergoing psychiatric treatment across the street, and she happened to be looking out the window. She was looking for "Mr. Clean," and nobody shaved their head in the '60s. And my hair was cut off almost completely, like it is now. And she spotted me and said, Oh my God, that's my Mr. Clean out there. And I was just on my way to lunch.

So she came over, and sure enough, she was the agent looking for Mr. Clean. I did a lot of promotional stuff. Flew to San Francisco. They had a parade. And I gave a check from Procter and Gamble to the mayor to clean up the city. They had Mr. Clean girls, and we'd show up at functions. There were a lot of shopping centers to open. I made a lot of money on that. I mean, it wasn't big money by today's standards, but it was enough to take it and start doing other stuff.

I started investing the money. Bought antiques. I became interested in leaded glass. Then I discovered Tiffany lamps. It was tremendously lucrative. That was back in the middle 1970s, when they were being discovered, and we bought and sold and bought and sold them. Tremendous profit in that. It was almost instantaneous.

I've been working on this house for twenty-five years. I do most of it with hand tools. I'm really fluid with tools. I'm a dentist. But I learned everything about craft—wood, plaster, stone—from the movie studios. I was working in the studios all the time I was in dental school. Acting and doing gripping, lighting, all kinds of trades. And I learned that forms come from nature, from seed buds germinating and blossoming out. Every curve can only go so far before it has to go the other way. You can see it on a snail shell. You can see it on the human body. The proportions have to be just so or they're not pleasing to the eye.

I just take the rotary handsaw and I can hold it straight. It could cut your hand off. But I have good facility with it. The first room that I did, the room we're sitting in, took me ten years.

For twenty years, I lived in Greenwich Village and worked in advertising as a rep for a film company in the cosmetic industry.

I had built my own home on Fire Island when I was twenty-six or twenty-seven, and it was like get out of New York Friday afternoon *really* fast before the crowd, run to the house, have company, stay on Monday morning, come back to New York and go back to work. One morning, I got up and thought about doing this for the rest of my life, and I didn't want to do it for the rest of my life.

At first, ten years ago, I tried commuting a bit. Here I was going from Greenwich Village, *on* twenty-four hours a day, to Sedona, where I'd go to sleep at 8:00 P.M. You don't ever call anybody after 9:00 P.M. here. And be up at 5:00 A.M. washing the car or something.

There's life here. Outside, I have property. There are animals and birds here. You can sit outside and hear them talk. You can go outside at night and see all the stars. That's real important, and it's more important than buying another pair of shoes.

There are crystals all over Sedona in the rocks. Quartz runs computers and watches and can be liquidized and has memory. The quartz crystals can absorb the energy from the sun, and you can bring them in your home and emit that life energy. It's a belief system that quartz crystals will energize and empower you with different thoughts. I believe this. If my computer is running on quartz, it's got to be doing something right. I don't understand it, but that doesn't mean I can't believe it. It is proven that crystals have a matrix system, which is a memory that gives off energy. Rocks and minerals all do things, same as plants.

Being here allows you to get away from the input. The noise, the subway, the buses, the fumes, the people. There's no pollution here. It's one of the cleanest places in America. Scientists have said that if there were a nuclear explosion, because of the configuration of the area, it would probably go right *over* us.

I've lived alone basically all my life. I like my space. If I want to get up in the middle of the night to move the furniture, I do. I've never had to ask another person permission to do anything.

Carole Mackler

Chika Sekiguchi

My father, ironically, was a country-western singer in Japan before he came here. I think that's how my parents met. She saw him playing in a café or something in a big hat and his cowboy boots and a guitar that had leather inlay and his name in it. He sang Hank Williams, mainly, and had a really nice voice. Now he's a graphic designer too, like me. So I take after my dad. My mom's a homemaker, but for the last five years she's been working at a boutique.

I was the firstborn over here. My older sister was born in Japan and was three when they came over. My father's just a real independent, freethinking person, and Japan was a little bit too stifling for his independence.

And I always sang, ever since I was little. My father would teach us all songs. We'd listen to Jackson Browne or Joni Mitchell. He would sing country songs. I'd always harmonize. We'd do these family things. And I kept playing the guitar and singing on my own in my bedroom, where no one could hear me.

I used to be a lot shyer than I am now. I mean, I was petrified to stand up in front of people and talk. I had to wear this big hat so no one could actually see me sing.

I think I've really changed in the last few years. I've had to discipline myself a lot more because I have a goal of making a CD. I've been saving every penny, which means I have almost no social life. I still feel like I'm in the postcollege stage. My furniture is all modular so it can be taken apart easily to move.

I just feel like, if I can make a living making music, that would be kind of a measure of success for me. But at the same time I know that it doesn't mean I'm doing *good* music. I spent all my years growing up analyzing everything about record jackets. Looking at all the photos. Part of that has faded a little bit, just because I've been in the business. But it's still there. I'm going to design my cover.

Chris Bradley

I'm the only one left on my side of the family. My grandfather made a great deal of money. Then he died, and my father, who was not very much of a businessman, took over the business. Then came the stock market crash in 1929, and that killed him. He lost everything. I was nineteen. I woke up in the morning the son of a millionaire, and by nightfall I had lost my father and everything else.

Of course I couldn't get a job. Who was going to hire somebody who doesn't know anything, anyway?

I had many friends in England, so I joined the Royal Air Force. When the war was over, I had friends in the UN and went to work there. I was part of a group that we don't talk about. An undercover sort of a thing.

When you're young it's easy. My health started to give way around Christmastime. My hip and then my knee, then angina, cataracts. All at once. I can hardly see. It's infuriating to me. These doctors are only interested in money. I've always been reasonably active. I'm locked up in the house. I can't drive anymore. I think I've lived too long.

All my old friends with the exception of perhaps two are dead.

I'm not scared of death. I've come close too many times. When I had my hip operated on, it was pretty nip and tuck. I had a spinal anesthesia, and oh, it was so peaceful. I could see a long tunnel and I could see the heavy part closest to me and I could follow it down almost to the end and I thought, Oh, it's so green and so peaceful, and then they had to go and bring me back. The grass was so green.

My memory is getting bad. I am aware of that. I have trouble keeping up with the days. If you don't have anything to do, the days just slip by and you don't pay any attention to it. You don't have anything to look forward to.

And here I am, living on pills. I'd rather live on steak and ale.

Dan Santow

I worked on *Oprah* for four months. Half of being a producer is finding and booking the guests. To book guests, you have to be somewhat disingenuous, no matter what they tell you. Because you want someone to come on the show. Most people are reluctant to go on TV, so there's all these arguments you use like: It will be cathartic for you. We said that all the time. I don't believe it. Or: It will help others. I don't believe that, either. And the best one is: You'll get to meet Oprah. *That* one I believe. And that's actually why a lot of people want to be on.

On Christmas you have to get Oprah gifts. She gets you gifts too. There was a big luncheon where you gave Oprah *your* gift and she gave you *hers*. She gave people cars and $10,000 trips around the world and *unbelievable* stuff. I had only been there eight weeks, so I wasn't expecting much, and she gave me a Bang & Olufsen stereo system. It was very fancy. It had this electric eye, like you walk towards it and this glass thing follows you. It was really modern, and I couldn't really figure out where to put it in my room. I gave her a very beautiful print by David Csicsko. One of the saints, and I framed it beautifully, and she claimed she liked it. It was St. Martin de Porres, the first black man canonized by the Catholic Church. And I did research and wrote an essay about him on the back. I thought it was a good gift.

I don't think she liked it. Actually, she said she liked it.

The summer between my senior year in high school and freshman year of college, I had my first boyfriend. Like major boyfriend. I met him at a gay juice bar in L.A. called the Odyssey. That's where I used to go when I was sixteen, seventeen. It was just great. It was one of the best things for my self-esteem as a young gay teenager to be able to be around all these kids who were just like me. So I had this boyfriend, my first ever boyfriend and one of only two Jewish boyfriends I've ever had.

So I was in this really great mood all summer.

And I wrote my brother a letter telling him that I was gay. And my brother was a member of the Revolutionary Communist Party then. So he wrote me this long letter back telling me that homosexuality was an outgrowth of capitalist economy and bourgeois society or something. Just the most ridiculous thing.

I remember thinking, He is out of his gourd.

Eddie Rouse

My introduction to heroin was my downfall. The high was—I felt like I was floating, everything was blissful, I closed my eyes and listened to jazz music. It was a release, you just let go. My whole life went in my veins. There's nothing like the high. It's the most dangerous drug I ever encountered in my life. I walked away from everything. Oh, man, I love heroin.

My ex and I ended up both doing heroin. We had a drugship. Our love was drugs.

I was working with campus police, but I ended up blowing it because I just didn't come to work. I was tired of it, anyway. I didn't really care anymore. Ended up living on the streets, her and I. She turned to prostitution. We lived off that for a while. Or we stole things, or we did whatever it took. We hustled. We would take dry wash (from drywall) and stuff it in vials. We'd go around during the day collecting the colored caps, putting them together, putting the drywall in, and selling them bundles at a time. Twenty a bag of crack. To go get our heroin. I been shot at, I been stabbed, I had my head cracked with a 9-mm.

I'm blessed. I should be dead. For all intents and purposes I should not be here. I wake up every day thinking that somebody's going to take it all away, that I don't deserve this. I've seen so many people die or be killed.

When I first came here, and got my life back, so to speak, I wasn't used to brushing my hair, washing my face, washing my clothes. I said, Damn, that takes a lot of work just to live from day to day. Just to get up in the morning. It's a lot of work. I didn't realize how far away I was from being in a routine, from being human. I did not care. Now, I had a spiritual awakening when I went to that mission. And I'm very grateful. I live right behind a mission, and what that reminds me of is that there is like ten yards difference between my apartment and that mission over there. It keeps reminding me that I'm only *that* far away from being right back where I started from.

This is the first time I lived alone in my entire life. It's scary. I never heard my own voice. I never woke up and there's nobody right beside me. Whatever I'm feeling is on *me,* I can't put it on no one. So I'm learning who I am. I get lonely, but I'm not alone, I've got me. Women complain I'm insecure and possessive. It's true. Women have always supported me. Sometimes the girl was out there selling her body to get drugs for both of us. I sold myself for drugs once. Once I allowed a man to go down on me. That's hitting bottom. You know.

The girl that was selling herself on the street like that. I never had a deeper love than her. I regret what drugs did, because I think we'd still be together. I've never had a better best friend. And I gave her her first shot of heroin.

Elaine Arata

Gene Kelly was always like, I loved him. That's the one guy I *did* actually write a letter to years ago—ten years ago, whatever. There was an article in the paper that he and Francis Ford Coppola were starting Zoetrope Studios. There's just something about Gene Kelly that I love. So I wrote him a note, and that was the first letter I've written to a celebrity. And I got a note back, and I was so thrilled that he wrote me back. It was typed out, but I think he signed it. Then I wrote him another note to thank him for writing me back because I was just so thrilled.

He said, Well, come down to the studio. So I went down to the set, and I was like, Oh my God, this is so great. At that point there was a lot of publicity because they had created Vegas indoors. Gene Kelly was supposed to be on the set because he was going to choreograph a movie.

So he came out, and I was going to go up and thank him, and say, Hi, do you remember me? I'm the one who wrote the letter.

But he looked so old and so feeble and his glasses looked like Coke bottle bottoms and I just didn't have the heart.

I was so disappointed, and I don't know why. I was just, oh my God. It broke my heart because in my mind he was this *picture*. I couldn't get past that. It was the first time I had seen a movie star or celebrity in person, and all the publicity photos are always of him young. And it made me just so sad. And there was this part of me that wanted to go up and thank him, but I just couldn't bring myself to go up to him.

I just kind of watched him.

It was sort of a surreal atmosphere because it was the "Vegas" set. And there were all these lights, and there were so many people around, and I just kind of stood there and I couldn't keep my eyes off him. I just watched him. Just watched him move around, watched him interact. And that's all I did. I don't know. I can't tell you how awful it was.

It was *sort* of like him still. He had this little gray hat on.

Elvira Alderman

I'm eighty-eight. I'm healthy. My husband died about ten years ago. Living alone is wonderful. It's great. I do as I want at the time I want to do it. I was happily married, to a certain extent.

In 1975, my husband bought me a car for myself. I wanted a convertible. This was after he made money. So he said, What kind of a car do you want? And I said, I'll look around. So I saw a Corvette, and I said, *That's* the car I want. He said, *What!* It costs as much as a Cadillac. Finally, I said, Let's go look at the Corvettes. He looked and saw that the resale values were better than what you got from the regular cars. So he broke down and bought me the car. It was nine thousand dollars in 1976. A blue one. I had that one until 1982.

Somebody stole it from the mechanic's garage and totaled it. So of course, I had to have another Corvette. Last year, I was stopped for the red light, and a little old lady came up and banged me from the back and totaled the car. The second one. She hit me with such force that the windshield cracked. I got a concussion and they took me to the hospital. I wanted another Corvette. This was 1995.

I got a red one. I wanted blue. But they didn't have one. I told them, I don't wear red, and I look much better in blue.

Enid Newfeld

In 1982, I injured an ankle. Every time I fell, they said, Wear a bandage on your ankle and your knee. Finally, I told the doctor, My foot is *not* swollen, but my knee's giving out. I went to a family doctor. He said, You're walking like you have multiple sclerosis. Sure enough. The MRI said mild. Just the one leg and the one arm. But then I had another attack.

There were times when I was in really good shape. I went to outpatient physical therapy. Once in a while, I'd have what they called an exacerbation. My knees would give out and I'd fall. And I was living alone. In October, my feet got to be like tree trunks. I tried to get out of bed, and I grabbed onto the wheelchair and it didn't hold me. I went down. They took me to Upstate. My son Stuart sent a package of chocolates. Fancy chocolates. My other son sent flowers when I was in the hospital.

The doctors don't know the cause, and they don't have the cure. And all the new medicines that sometimes work and sometimes don't work, they're extremely, extremely expensive. It's a thousand dollars a month, and you have to inject yourself. I could not do that. I'm on Social Security disability and Medicare, but not Medicaid. So I have to pay my own prescriptions out of my pocket. I have to pay for my aides out of my pocket. The one wheelchair is on Medicare, the other one I had to buy for five thousand dollars. It's mobile and it's electric.

I cry a lot. I've got Zoloft. I don't think it's helping. I've been seeing a psychologist. He had me write a letter about how things are and how you would like them to be. And he read it and said, This is very, very negative. I said, Yes, it is. He said, Isn't there anything positive happening to you? I said no. I hate living here. I am far away from everything and everybody I know. I'd like to go to the warm weather.

Your emotions are all unstable with MS. Your head is messed up because of the plaques. I now have a lot more than the original three. Denial. Denial. I've been depressed for many years. Depression could be caused by the MS or by other things. My daughter asked the doctor, Can you get my mother to stop screaming? And I said, Linda, I've been screaming at you all my life! Why are you telling me it's MS? Have I had MS all my life? I'm a screamer. The opposite of my husband. He'd say, When you're finished screaming, we'll talk. And then I'd go inside and slam the door. Never threw anything, though.

I'm going to have another birthday the end of February. The last one really depressed me because it was the big six-oh. I'm afraid I'm going to end up in a nursing home.

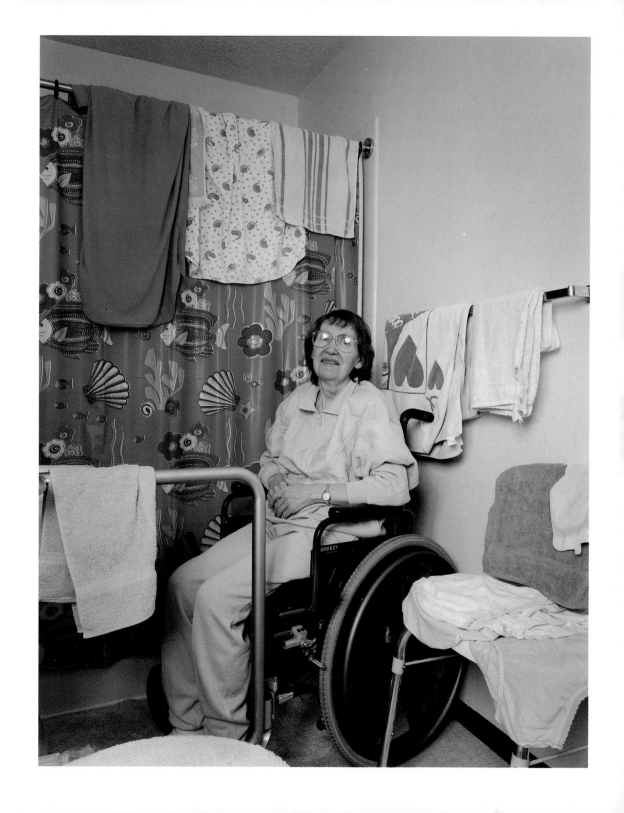

Eva Wulkan

I left Berlin in 1936. You could still use public transportation then. You could still go to the coffeehouses. They had big signs, "Jews, Go to Paris," which, if they would have let us, that wouldn't have been such a bad thing. It's not so bad, people said, because business was very good, even the Jews said that, because Hitler was rebuilding and doing all these super-highways.

It took about two years to get a visa for my mother to get to the Dominican Republic. This was 1941. She was all set, she had all the papers. On that one particular Sunday, the day before the Monday when my mother would have left, I got a telegram, Travel Impossible. Mother. And that was the end. Hitler had made a law that Saturday. He liked to make laws on weekends because the international papers weren't as alert. She was sent to Auschwitz, and that was the end of that.

My husband died twelve years ago. We were happy together for a long time. But then not later. In the end, he was very moody and suspicious. Somebody would call, and I would talk, and he would say, Who did you talk to? Did she call or did you call? Why did you talk so long? Suspicious of every little detail. Basically, he loved me too much, you know? He noticed that I didn't love him anymore. But he punished me more and more. Completely ignoring me, not talking to me.

On the day he died, it was my brother's birthday. So my husband said to him on the phone, "I wish you a better year than the last." Those were the last words I heard from him. And on this day he committed suicide. And that was it. And he chose the day of my brother's birthday because he knew how close I was to my brother. He drank half a bottle of whiskey, which he never drank, and then he took a lot of pills.

I had only been gone an hour. I called the police, fire department, and they came and brought an ambulance. He had tried it once before, five or six years before. He became depressed when he was eighty years old. He didn't want to get old.

I was in Vietnam in 1969 and 1970. Two tours. The first job I did was in personnel management. You keep the records of all the people and their promotions. But that was too boring, so a couple friends of mine and I decided to join the First Cavalry Division. That's with the helicopters. We signed up to be door gunners. It's like you're in the door of the helicopter, and when they're flying to pick up people, you're right there in the open and you got an M-60 machine gun and if someone's firing at you, you fire back. There is a six-week life expectancy of door gunners. I did it for a year. Only got hit twice. Even when I got hit, it was just flesh wounds. I wasn't scared. It seemed safer than being on the ground. I was nineteen.

I don't think I'd fight in another war. It wasn't so much the war itself, 'cause I thought we was right, but it was the government. The government wouldn't let us bomb places where we knew we should be bombing. They held us back.

I was twenty-four when I first got married. Had a daughter. She's nineteen or twenty now. I haven't seen her in years. She used to live with me when I first moved out here. Her mother and I were divorced. I kind of wish she'd have stayed and finished high school. Went on to college. I had plans for her to go to college or whatever. I tried to help her out the best I could. But she decided she wanted to live with her mother. Now she's like working at McDonald's or something in Missouri.

You see more strange things around here than anywhere. When I was working at Chrysler, nights, you'd get off around midnight. Me and this other guy would ride motorcycles home from work side by side. One time we seen something in the sky, and we both stopped our bikes and looked at each other. And then rode on. We never discussed it or nothing. We just went on. It was a strange light up there, seen it for a little bit and then it's just gone.

I seen some strange things out here. I'm not saying I seen like spaceships or anything. This is strange. My brother told me he used to go out looking for UFOs. When I moved out here, he said, "Don't go looking for them or they'll look for you."

He got the feeling that they were following him.

Gordon Harrington

I got involved in politics at Cornell during the anti–Vietnam War movement. I hooked up with Marxists who were very serious about organizing beyond the campus. In working-class communities. So I moved to Chicago with a group of people just after I graduated. I spent six years doing labor organizing in different kinds of factories for shop-floor issues like health and safety but also organizing for socialism and for serious structural change in society.

We wanted to end the government and end capitalism as such. We were socialists. We were Marxist-Leninists. It was a Maoist-Marxist movement in the '70s, and we were very partial to the People's Republic of China and its politics. After I left, this group went on to form a new American Communist party.

I was never a real successful comrade. I was always doubting things and wanting to read things and investigate things, and I was never as enthusiastic as I should be. I was always what we used to call a petit bourgeois vacillator. I never served on any committees, and I never got to go to China. I was always at the bottom of the heap. I was always trouble. But, ironically, I was always one of the best organizers because I got along with people. I tried to deal with people based on where *they* were coming from rather than where *we* were coming from. Speak to them so that it made sense in their own lives. I organized quite a few members into this group.

I also felt as though I wasn't as dedicated as some of the other people. I just didn't like getting up at 4:30 in the morning when it's twenty below so you could drive an hour to hawk your left-wing newspaper in front of a steel mill and sell maybe ten or fifteen copies in two hours. I couldn't get enthusiastic about that, but I did it. Reluctantly. And I'd make snide remarks all the way down—but you're not supposed to make snide remarks. You're supposed to be an agent of the working class and all this stuff.

It was cultish in some ways.

It's been real hard at times since my wife and I separated. At times, I really enjoy being by myself. It's nice to live knowing you're not hurting somebody every single day. I had left once before for two or three months back at Princeton. And then I came back. This time we were just having a lot of problems. We were dancing the same dance over and over. We couldn't seem to solve anything. We tried. We went to counseling for several years. But the differences just seemed irreconcilable and she sort of precipitated the break, but I didn't do a whole lot to resist it. In some ways, I think she did me a favor because I would have probably just plodded along and hung on just 'cause I didn't want to be a failure.

Harvey Teres

Hector Rodriguez

My dream is to live off my paintings. Then maybe save some money and go on a trip somewhere.

When I graduated, I had this idea that *I was an artist* and that I was more intelligent and more talented than anyone else. See, I believe it for about three weeks; then for two weeks, I'm like the worst thing in the world, and the next three weeks I'm amazing. I go through those phases.

But since I'm young, I try to think I'm special and better. I went through a phase that, even though I was not convinced of it, I wanted to think that maybe I was the second coming of Jesus Christ. So, for a while I was trying to make miracles and stuff, but it never worked.

And so I thought, Maybe I'm the anti-Christ, and then I started getting scared and thinking, I'm the anti-Christ, what can I do? But then I thought, Oh, this is bullshit.

I thought I was an alien for a while, and then I thought my parents were not my real parents. Stuff like that. Not to the point where I needed to go to a psychiatrist or anything. Sort of like I was playing, but trying to make it real, like in a Superman story.

I was sort of going out with this woman for a while. She used to be a model at clubs and stuff like that. And they had transvestites. She had transvestite friends. And she was telling me how they taught her all these tricks. Like, she doesn't have big breasts, and so they gave her tips of how to make her breasts look larger, besides just wearing those bras that pull all your body up here. And she was telling me how she wore makeup if she is wearing a low-cut kind of thing. She paints shadows to make her breasts look round.

I thought it was so interesting that the person I was going out with was using tricks a transvestite gave to her to look a certain way. And she used those tricks to go out with me.

Jeanne Williams

My parents were very critical. In many ways I didn't feel like I had a childhood. I was always aware of the tremendous sacrifices they made for me. My parents were not the most demonstrative of people. They didn't tell you they loved you. They weren't overly touchy-feely. They weren't overly affectionate with each other.

My parents were both incredibly willing to sacrifice everything for us. My mother would go without so that we would have. That kind of sacrifice. They both are that way. So I felt that they were doing good things for me, and that's why it made it hard to be angry at them. How could I be angry at these people who do so much for me? I am angry with them. There's a lot of anger in me. I'm a very angry person. When you first meet me, everybody puts on their good face. Nice, easygoing. But as a teenager and a young adult, I was very dark. Very depressed, very detached.

I wanted to be good, I wanted to be the best. I always remember from a very early age wanting to be intensely competitive. Not with other people, but with myself. If I was good enough at something, my parents would notice it. My parents just took it for granted. They were not complimenters. Because they wanted to raise modest children.

I wanted to drop out of law school after my first year. Just because I hated it. And I was doing well. Solid student. I wanted to be a director or a director of photography in the movie business. I was always fascinated by images and telling stories. And I was a huge reader. I love stories. My parents taught me that if you're black, you have to be twice as good. Nobody is going to take care of you, no one is going to marry you. You're not going to be little Susie home-maker. My mother always worked, there was always the expectation that I would work. So they told me to do something practical where there was stability and you have money and you don't have to worry about those sorts of things. That meant being a doctor, lawyer, in business. The arts were too risky. It's fine to explore and have fun with but nothing to take too seriously. Plus nobody they knew was in movies.

Now I'm an agent. I work primarily in television. But I also represent writers and directors. People who write and direct movies for features and television.

You can't be *old* in this business. They don't think there is any wisdom in being older. In Hollywood being old means you don't know what's hip anymore. It doesn't mean you have insight or depth of experience.

Jennifer Crisafulli

My life is not normal.

I'm an assistant photography editor at a rock-and-roll magazine, so I'm around famous people all day. You go on photo shoots, and then you become friends with them. I do, anyway, because I have that personality. I can pretty much relate to the more obscure, odd ones. Whether they think they're odd, or they want to be odd, or some of them truly are just mad. Whatever it is, everyone is an egomaniac.

I primarily hang out with music people. I go out every night, but I try to be home by 5:00 A.M. so I can get to work by 10:00. It is the most insane thing when you're sitting there and you're all fucked up with your friends, who are celebrities. The shit that people come up with. You're trying to have a conversation with them, and strange people come up with different lines like Hey man, do I know you from somewhere? You look familiar. Are you . . . ? And they'll make up a name. And you know damn well, 'cause the guy's been stalking you for half an hour, sitting there watching, and he *knows* who you are.

People say, Well then, celebrities shouldn't go into public places if they don't want to be bothered. Well, fuck that. Why can't the public just learn to ignore them? Why can't the public have some sort of cool understanding?

You really get that feeling that everyone wants a piece of the action. It's not just the talent that's egomaniacs, everyone's a fucking egomaniac that's around these people. Or that wants to be around.

I'm a little bit more aware of my sexuality. I know it works, but it's not the reason why I do it. If I think I have to use my sexuality, or if I think I have to show a guy my cleavage or a bartender at a bar, I become skeeved right away. And I won't do that. So instead, if I'm there, I won't hang over the bar and show my tits, I will actually use my sexuality in a cold, hard way—like, Here it is and don't even fucking look at me.

I won't let my walls down. I am this character that I've built myself to be, that I truly *am* at this point. But the real me would probably like to be running through a field innocently picking flowers and putting them in my boyfriend's hair.

But people are attracted to this character I've now created and they love it.

Jessica Tuck

As an actor, your emotions are very exposed.

One of the things that attracted me to acting was you could, behind a mask, entertain people. You could really let go, and you weren't necessarily held accountable for what you were doing because it was the character, not you. So there was a great deal of freedom.

When I was on a soap opera, I was in people's living rooms five days a week, and in my case for three and a half years. And people are as addicted to you as an actor as to the silly little story. They live vicariously through you. And they get an idea of who you are in their heads, and when they see you on the streets, I mean, I used to walk down the streets in New York and someone would recognize me as Megan off of *One Life to Live*. They never called me Jessica, they would say *Megan*, and they'd have all these questions about me. There was this whole life that I wasn't even leading that was in their head that they constructed for me. I could get into restaurants faster. People always wanted to do things for me. And it made me so uncomfortable. Because I thought, *You don't know who I am*. You're treating me as if I'm this person you've constructed. And I'm not special because of this. There are other things I want you to think of me as special for.

I would love to get on a good TV series. To have a regular gig on TV gives you a lot of freedom financially as well as in terms of your time. The way it works now is, I get a job, and it ends, and then I'm looking for the next one. And so it's hard to do things with my life because when I'm not working, I'm unemployed. And when I'm working, I can't go anywhere. I'm really good about saving money. The minute I get a job, in my mind I go, Okay, a certain percentage of this is going away in my long-term savings. I always, in my head, treat it like it's the last job I'll ever have.

When you're an actress, you're not allowed to have your period. You're not allowed to be bloated. You're not allowed to have cramps. You're not allowed to have a sad day when something happens in your life. You can't gain a pound. I refuse to be anorexic and thin. Too bad. This is what they get. The one thing I *do* do, is I have these mastectomy boobs that I got from a store for women who've had mastectomies that I wear to auditions so it looks like I have big, bouncy boobs. Because I wouldn't have plastic surgery. If they want big, bouncy boobs, I'll give them to them, but I'll just take them out when I'm done. Fuck that. It gets hard. That's why you've got to have other things in your life that you define yourself by. If this is what defines you, then what are you when you're not working?

Lee died four years ago. It was really difficult. Because not only have I changed since I met Lee when I was nineteen, but the world has changed. Dating has changed. It's like being in a time capsule and coming back to some strange land. Only the racy girls had sex then. You saved it for marriage. My generation of women got married very young, so we were inexperienced. Very much so. The sexual revolution certainly passed us by. Unfortunately.

I went from really nice parents who took care of me to a marriage where my husband took care of me. I'd only been treated well, and I didn't realize that there were people who had different types of relationships and different ways of treating people. It was a shock. I was hurt very badly. I was in a relationship for about ten months with a breakup in between. In retrospect, while it ended poorly, when it was going on, it was very exciting. And it was passionate and fun, having been just the second person in my entire life that I'd been with. I was rather swept off my feet, as a matter of fact. All my life I had lived a very closed, cloistered, protected life.

No one loves going out more than me. I love going to the theater and symphonies and nice dinners and dressing up. I love being on the go. I enjoy women's company, but I don't like hanging out with them all the time. I like men. I really like men. I like male companionship. I like the way they think. I like everything about them.

I went out with a yacht captain. He was cute looking, but not much substance. And he had a hard time paying for a light bite of dinner and a movie. Unless someone can take me out for a really pleasant evening, I don't want to downgrade. I'm very fortunate to have a really nice lifestyle, and I would expect that someone would have one somewhat similar to me.

I do know a lot of women out there who buy their men cars, studios. There's a lot of women my age that to have someone, they *have* to do this. Thank God I have not been confronted with that. It's depressing. It's just the same where a lot of women stay in marriages where they know their husbands have mistresses. But what do they have if they divorce? They aren't Mrs. Da-da-da. They don't have the house. In many cases, the wives are very aware, but have made a life of sorts. And I think women, certainly fifty and over, are very wary and frightened of what their life will be without this figurehead husband. What will they have? They'll have a life of loneliness, eating alone. At least they have the aura of being Mrs. Whatever.

Since my husband passed away, I'm much more knowledgeable on the ways of the world.

Joan Cohen

Joan Harrison

My mother was hilarious. I remember once we were driving somewhere in the Country Squire with like thirteen kids, and this guy next to us was excavating his nostrils, digging away, so my mother rolled down her window, and he rolled down his. And she said, "Pick me a winner!" and she zoomed off. And she had thirteen kids in hysterics for hours.

I grew up in this Jewish enclave in a blue-collar town on Long Island. We were the weird family. The family with a station wagon in pieces on the front lawn, lots of political posters festooning the portico. Kids running around with dirty hair and dirty teeth. When the hygienist came to the school and asked who didn't brush their teeth today, I knew what was coming, and sure enough my brother Wayne's hand shot up, and he said, "I *never* brush my teeth." It was quite a family.

My mother was really an inventive, fabulous mother. Until she fell apart. When my dad got sick, she didn't take it well. I was eight. My dad was much older than my mother. Never really earned a living. My father had a bad heart, many heart attacks, and he had a kidney removed. Lots of postop infections. He had a bypass.

She eventually opened a little bed and bath store she called Shower City. We called it Sour Shitty. It was an indoor flea market. It wasn't exactly high-class seeing your mother selling vinyl toilet seats.

I started coming into my own in high school when I realized I was smart and if I'd just apply myself, I would do just great. Which happened. I applied to Penn, and sure enough they gave me a full scholarship. It was my deliverance, completely. And I'm very indebted to that school now, and I do a lot of work for them. They saw something in me that I really didn't know I had. And they were right, I suppose.

Now I'm the vice president of miniseries at CBS. I buy projects that run two or more nights, four or more hours. I oversee the scripting and the development. It tends to be the crème de la crème of television. I think some of the best stuff produced is in the miniseries format. I'm in constant production. It's very exciting. I love my job. I think TV is a much maligned medium, and I do think there is brilliant television on just about every night of the week. Now granted there's a lot of shit on too. But I do watch. I enjoy it.

I'm pretty systematized in general. I'm an efficiency expert. I'm very well groomed. I'm probably a little overgroomed. I might be. I might spend a little too much time nit-picking. I like keeping myself attractive. I wasn't particularly attractive—I was a downright unattractive twenty-something. I was dumpy, my face was fat. Lots of people tell me I get better looking with age, and I think it's true.

Joe Blaustein

We were so close that my friends used to accuse us of being insular. She died eleven years ago. She was a gorgeous, wonderful, natural-type woman. We were really linked. She got breast cancer at the age of forty.

As you can see, I can't get over it. She was so strong, and she did so well that she survived six years, and I thought that she was fine but then she metastasized as bone cancer and then the next four years were very difficult. But she was a tough woman and never complained, and she was really quite beautiful, too. She had that natural look to her. Hardly used makeup. Just some eye makeup. Didn't do the Hollywood-hair routine. She just pulled it back in a ponytail and just exuded this beauty. She had a gift. She understood nature. We wound up in our little enclave. We had thirty to forty animals at one time. And we had wonderful kids.

We were rare from what I know from our friends. She thought I was the greatest lover in the world. I thought it was only because of her that I was that way. We knew how to just satisfy and please each other in so many ways that we were just unbelievable.

When death was imminent, we decided to go for a weekend up the coast to Santa Barbara and get a place that we had years ago on the ocean, just to hear the water. This was ten or eleven years ago. It was like saying good-bye—sexually and physically—and we made love in our usual way. She enabled me to *be* somebody because of the way she was. I'd feel her reaction and I would react. We were like teenagers, and we wound up, we made love, it sounds like bragging, but you know, several times. There was an old train that goes by in Santa Barbara, and it was two in the morning, and the train— It was out of a corny movie, she was climaxing and the train was going by and she said, Twenty-eight years and I still hear the train.

I know there are dangers inherent in living alone, like you know you could get really strange. You can feel like you're haunting the fucking place sometimes.

Judd Hostetler

I was in bookkeeping and statistics for twenty-two years, and I felt very unhappy in my job. The only thing that kept me going was my volunteer work—Junior Achievement in the late '50s, Boy Scout work in the '60s, tutoring in the '70s, taking care of mother in the '80s. I always got involved in volunteer work.

My boss, who was thirty years younger than me, was getting impatient because I wasn't learning the computers quick enough, so one day I just stood up and did a somersault in midair from a standing position. I had never done it before. I smashed my leg, but I didn't *say* anything and I didn't *hit* anybody. Well, it scared the people, because I had always been so mild mannered. I was dismissed the next day. Here I had been working all these hours for the company without being paid overtime. Twenty-two years. Fired.

I began working with Meals on Wheels as the coordinator and driver in 1990. Finally, the next spring, I was recognized for what I had been doing at the senior center. Lo and behold, in April my name was submitted for the Senior Man of the Year. I was overwhelmed. I have the citation back here. It was a highlight of my life. I was interviewed, and they wrote me up. And they said, This is a fun person. Even then I liked dancing. It was something new that I was already doing once in a while.

I'm scared of sharp-edged things. I have been for all my life. Oh, like scissors and knives and saws. A psychiatrist felt it was my fear of sex, my fear of relationships. I cut out my newspaper articles with that black notebook divider. It's probably faster than scissors, anyway. I never risked a relationship. I'm still a virgin. And I haven't had more than two dates with a woman until Carol came into my life in my sixty-fourth year.

For forty-two years I've done calisthenics twenty minutes a day. The other day I built it up to four miles. I walk back and forth in the house. To go from the garage door in the kitchen to the far bathroom, back, and a second round trip, I can do in one minute. That's 265 feet. Well, I just extended that. Forty round trips is a mile. Forty times two is eighty. If I do three of those twenty-minute walks, that's three miles. And of course I don't do more than a mile at a time. I take off my sweater. I don't have to put on galoshes. I can listen to Beethoven's Sixth. Or I can listen to rhythm and blues. Four miles is 160 round trips of my house.

My parents were everybody else's grandparents' age, and I knew that they weren't going to be around into my late life. And that bothered me a lot. Everything's like a precious quantity. I make things precious quantities.

Writing in my journal is like the jail of habit. It will be twenty years around now. It's a barbell. Because what if I die? Everybody I love would get hurt if they read that stuff. And I don't want that. I really would like a big bonfire. Sometimes I wonder what I was doing in 1979 on this day, and I can look it up, and I get taken back to a million different feelings. And I think, That was *me*? I remember that, and I *hate* remembering it. It's an amazing document, but it's really scary.

I get up, have my coffee, sit at whatever morning area I've got, and roll a cigarette and light a couple candles. Ritual. Sometimes three hours will go by. I can honestly say that it isn't exactly beneficial—it can take small feelings and make them too big. It's a way to say something about someone when I wouldn't want to burden anybody else with the details. Nobody would have the patience to listen to anything like that. And they shouldn't.

Love and awareness of mortality. They're inseparable. The proof of something. We have to have that coexistence. Any moment something could destroy something. That's a real weird thing for me. I couldn't care less about my own dying. The only thing I would feel bad about was that it would make a few people feel sad. If I preceded my mother's death, it would kill her. My brother would miss me terribly.

My biggest challenge is loving something in spite of that minefield walk. Not making everything so fucking precious to the point where you're frozen.

In undergraduate school, my parents sent me Syrian bread. Which is gold. Homemade Syrian bread and pepperoni. And I was saving it for that *right time,* and that fucking bread got green and fuzzy. I saved it until it was no good anymore. Special bread, you know. It's silly. It's defeating. That stands out because, it should have been a perfect example of the futility and waiting for the exact right moment for something.

And I still haven't learned. My mom sends me crosswords and notes, and I save the fucking piece of paper that says, "Here's the crossword puzzles, honey."

It's proof.

Jude Lewis

Kirby Majer

I always heard stories about what the concentration camps were like. I heard about where my dad was, where my mother was, where my aunts and uncles were. I always saw it, but I didn't necessarily *feel* it. I've had a fairly good life. We've always had food on the table—you know, things like that.

And my dad brought us up never to blame anybody. That was the past. My mother got pissed in high school when one of my girlfriends was German. And that really bothered her. Years later, I went to a concentration camp, and I took like thousands of pictures, and I knew I could show them to my dad but not to my mother. So I asked him if he wanted to see them and he said, "No, why would I want to see those pictures? *I still see it.* I don't need to see what it looks like today."

The thing that bothers me the most about this happened outside of Munich in Dachau. What bothered me was that I wanted to go there and see it, and I was less than four blocks from the place and I stepped in this little restaurant asking for directions. And I'm asking about the concentration camp, and I even said it in German, and these people had no idea what I was talking about. And that sort of made me rethink a lot of these issues.

When I was a kid I felt that no matter what problem I had, it didn't compare to what happened to my parents. My dad was once running away and this guy was going to shoot him, shot twice and missed him. So no matter how bad, if I had a bad professor in school, I couldn't come home and say anything. Because of that, I was very mature as a young kid and went through a very unmature phase later, even now.

I was much more of an adult as a kid than maybe I am now. I know it had an effect, but I'm not sure how or what.

I feel like before I can cry, I've got to lose three limbs and an eye.

My basic thing is *work* is the law of the universe. I understand that you have to work, you have to be productive. Basically, I think there are few sorts of employment situations you could put yourself in that are going to be ideal, so pick one, and trudge through it.

I don't *love* industrial relations. I'm going to be successful at doing it. No subject, no profession really interests me that much. Any idiot can pursue a career and get to the top if they understand what they need to value to get there. I'm not very impressed with most things. Risk isn't something that I was accustomed to taking.

I think civil war is coming. A lot of it will be dictated on this welfare-reform thing. I work, and I'm not pro-welfare, either. But you're going to see anarchy. Because these are people who have no concept of the value of work. Free ride, easy living. I can go rob easier than I can get a job. I think you'll see the drug trade get even more malicious.

You know what's going on with the inner cities? The crime and what not? When they take it out of the Robert Taylor homes and bring it down on Michigan Avenue? They're going to do that because it's only going to take one person. Farrakhan could be the one to set it off. I mean, look at what happened with the Rodney King thing and the riots. All it's going to take is one precipitating event. It's going to take one person to bring the hoodlums together, so to speak. Now you have gangs getting political, and a lot of people tie that to what the Mafia used to do. It's scary. You have the man Farrakhan going over to meet with brother Qadhafi, who trains terrorists, and you have all these well-armed people who have *no* value for life. Farrakhan infiltrates prisons, and that's where he gets a lot of his people.

I think you have to worry about Farrakhan. He's really set himself up to be a martyr because, if he keeps doing these sorts of things, he's going to get assassinated. Farrakhan's been setting up for years that the government is having a plot to assassinate him. To do the sorts of things that he's doing, he's asking for it, you know? He's going to go out like a martyr.

This will happen in my lifetime. I think it could jump off in two years. I think it could be twenty.

Lance Bean

I was born in an artists' colony in California. My father named me Lisa Danielle so that when I became a famous artist I would have a nice name.

I do these Western still life setups. What people put on their walls is what the window of their soul really wants to look out at. Maybe it's a ranch, maybe it's horses, or sky with nothing in it. I have always wanted to live on a ranch and have a horse. When you don't have children, you want to leave something behind that will make the world a nicer or more complete place than if you hadn't been here.

After twenty years of marriage, I split up from my husband three and a half years ago. We were both so angry and drained. We collected guns, and it was quite possible that it would come to a shoot-out in the street one day, and I had no qualms that it could as easily been me pulling the gun as him.

He would go through periods where he wouldn't speak to me. I think the longest was four months. I knew when it was going to be a long, drawn-out one because he would start closing the bedroom door, which meant I was supposed to move to the couch or the studio to sleep, and he took all the food in the refrigerator that I bought and he put it on one side and then he would go out and buy a duplicate gallon of milk, head of lettuce, cans of tuna—his cold cereal would be next to my cold cereal. His dish and plate would be kept separate from mine as if I was going to contaminate his silverware, and we would live like that for anywhere from a few days to four months at a time.

I finally left him and rented a two-bedroom little house. I had really strong beliefs about family and commitment. If you go by the Bible literally, you're basically supposed to live the life of Christ. And if it comes to laying your life down for a commitment rather than figure out a way to get out of the bad part, the Christian way is to lay down your life and make the sacrifice. But somehow I just felt like I had laid down my life and laid down my life until there was no life left. It used to be if anybody ever said they were divorced, I used to put them into a category, Oh there's somebody that broke a commitment, there's somebody that failed at something. And now when I see somebody who's divorced I think, There's somebody who had the courage to make a change and live with it.

At first I was scared and guilt-ridden. I've been living on a ranch for two years, and I hope by summer I'm going to have my own little ranch. It's only an acre and a half, but I've got two horses and the two cow dogs.

Lisa Danielle

Lisbeth Ungar

My sister and I came over from Vienna in November 1939. Our parents were under the impression that it would all blow over. We were always optimists, somehow. It was the Jewish approach. Even in camps, people had a certain amount of optimism, and some *did* survive. You cannot defend against a machine gun. My parents said, Don't worry, they won't do anything to us.

Just to go out on the street in Vienna was dangerous. There was not a store you could run to for protection. If they shoot you on the street, you couldn't do anything. Every step was misery. Misery. Then we had to go to the Gestapo. We had to pay punish tax. We had to pay tax on the money we left there. Do I have to tell you more? The most outrageous things you can think of, they used and they applied. You know when I talk about it, I live through it again. And I was lucky!

My sister and I took any jobs that were available when we got here. I was a mother's helper, I was a maid. It was 1939, the tail end of the Depression. I had a job for five dollars a week. For me and my sister, it was an adventure.

I ask myself, How come I'm here a survivor for the second time? I have Hitler, and now I survive my poor husband and my poor sister. Far too few were as fortunate as I was. There is a guilt, yes, absolutely. A guilt feeling complex on the survivors because they're constantly asking, How come we were saved and six million were not?

I was married for forty-six years. My poor husband died. He had a heart attack and a little stroke, but he recuperated fully. He was able to drive again. But within six months— I still claim it was a stroke. They said it was cardiac arrest. Here at the table, at dinner, he collapsed. The ambulance came right away, of course, and they couldn't revive his heart. So they took him to the hospital next door. They had the heart started to beat again, but his brain was gone. I begged. I'd take him back under *any* circumstances. They said, You cannot, you cannot. It will be ten years. And my poor sister died two days later. She had heart trouble. Two days later.

You have to pay a price for getting old, there is no doubt. You don't have the energy, the strength to do things. I drop things. One is shocked at this. I do my best not to be a burden to myself, and not to burden, God forbid, my sons. They are very good, they are attentive. I can't praise them enough.

I am lonely. On the other hand, there are millions of women like I am. And they can manage. And I have to learn to do it, too. You have to learn to accept misery at times. That's life. I live comfortably. I can read. I can walk. I have friends, but the circle is shrinking.

Lorin Adolph

I always loved, not so much food, but to be in the kitchen. I'd have friends come over when I was in grammar school, and we'd go to the Jewel and buy a cake mix. We'd garnish it with maraschino cherries and we'd goop frosting on. Nothing was homemade, it was out of a box, but just the *idea* of doing it, I think I always loved. I went to cooking school right out of high school.

I started by catering—cooking in clients' homes. I'd bring all of my equipment with me: my pasta maker, ice cream maker, knives, sheet pans. I was making very good money doing it. I could have made more money if I'd known to mark up when I rented plates. And I never charged a fee for me.

But for me it was the *food,* and I was so excited that people were letting me do this. I would go to the markets every day. I made a lot of homemade pasta. You could always tell where I'd been because my footprint was a box of Quaker cornmeal 'cause I dry out the pasta on cornmeal.

I did that for about five or six years. It was very hard work. I was twenty-one years old and living in this world that wasn't *my* world. I had a client who had the largest collection of Kenneth Noland's work. All these fabulous lives and artwork and furniture. Amazing. I was very impressed by all that. They were shopping at Ultimo, so *I* wanted to shop there. They're going to this benefit, *I'll* go to that benefit. And I thought these people were my friends. And I realized that they weren't. They were my clients. Some of them were friendly, but I'd see them the next day walking down the street, and they wouldn't even know who I was.

Now I'm a private chef. My schedule always changes, so my week is never boring. One week I'll work five days in a row. This week I'm off five days in a row. I'm given free rein of a menu. I can go to the store and buy whatever I want, make any dish I want and just be creative. I call one of my boss's assistants and ask how many people for dinner tonight. Sometimes, it's just him. Sometimes, he doesn't want anybody over. And I'll serve him a three-course meal. Since he's been divorced, my job description has changed, by my own doing. I realized after a while, the napkins were ten years old and there was no one to replace them, so now I will buy things. I just bought some beautiful lacquer trays the other day and served stir-fry on them. And I buy candles and vases.

This guy is so busy. And I want to make his life a little more beautiful.

Mary-Louise Diggs

When I was coming up, I had a really hard time. My father was brown-skinned, my mother was very light. My parents didn't talk about their backgrounds very much. They would always say, Forget it. We knew that my grandmother was four years old when the slaves were freed. We just read between the lines because they never talked about it at all. When we went to school, I had some very, very dark-skinned friends, and there were a lot of the real dark-skinned people who did not like light-skinned people. There were also light-skinned people who did not like dark-skinned people. And I hate to tell you, it still goes on. It still goes on. We were brought up in a very strict place. My parents did not teach us to hate anyone, whether you were white, black, yellow, green, or what. We loved everybody. I brought my daughter up the same way. She lives in Brookville, Maryland. They live predominately with different nationalities. It made no difference to us. But I went to the Episcopal school for three years, I had no trouble there. But when we started going to public school . . .

I'm very sensitive about my complexion. I guess I'm so anxious for everybody to like me that I will go out of my way. One of the greatest things you can show a person is a smile.

I am not prejudiced at all. I can look at the KKK, and I don't like what they're doing. But God says, Love everybody, so I love everybody. I try to be friendly to everybody because it's just one of those things. He made us all.

I have some good friends who are dark-skinned. But I will find one or two people who will look at me as if to say, Who does she think she is? They have not been what you would say *mean,* but just the look, you can tell.

I had a brother who was brown. My grandmother was brown. My aunt was light. My mother was light, my father was light brown. I have a cousin in Brooklyn who's dark brown. And really we all got along just fine together.

Mel White

I got married in my early twenties. We were childhood sweethearts. We got married in 1964, and it was a year and a half later when we discovered that she had multiple sclerosis. Normally, it doesn't progress that fast, but hers was rather rapid. Kind of like straight downhill. She would have periods of remission, but they wouldn't last long. And then she transcended in August of 1970.

We brought her body back down here from New Rochelle for the funeral. We decided we were not going to have anybody in black—the pallbearers would not be in black, we would ask the ushers and flower girls to wear colorful dresses and suits of any color. One of the sisters-in-law had on a colorful dashiki. Big Afro. My mother-in-law was in a powder blue suit. My mom was in a pink suit. And that service became more like a bon voyage. And it wasn't so final, and there wasn't all this heavy sadness, crying and weeping.

Einstein said that energy is never lost, it just changes its form. There has to be some sort of spiritual transition at the time of so-called death. The body was in fact a shell, it was a vehicle for something much more important than flesh and blood. When it's no longer useful, it goes back to the ground from whence it came. And then the spirit moves on into wherever we think spirits go.

I believe in reincarnation. Not in the sense of recognizing someone physically from a prior life, but acknowledging a kinship in your spirit from many lives. We meet people, and we have this special affinity with that person. We don't understand what it is. We think we just *like* them. And a lot of times it's just some acknowledgment of some past experiences.

I enjoy my space. This is my sanctuary. There's a lot of stuff that goes on outside of that door. We have to earn a living, we have to travel, we have to eat, we have to do a million things. But if there's anyplace in the world that we should be able to *stop* and have a moment of peace, it should be home.

Michael Ingbar

Years ago I got involved in a very, very controversial philosophy called Scientology. Dianetics. I've been involved in it since 1970. I've done almost everything you can do in Scientology. I've gotten 90 percent of the counseling available at all of the levels. There are only about a thousand people who have done the things I've done in Scientology.

In Scientology, we believe that in order to become truly an individual, and be who you are without getting everybody pissed off at you, you have to be able to heighten your ability to be aware of other people. If you think about this, it's a very simple concept. Ethics in Scientology is defined as contemplation for optimum survival.

It's expensive. But if you compare the cost of a course compared to college tuition, it's very cheap. Because in college you go to school for a certain period of time, you're paying for time, you're not paying for the *benefit* you get out of it. When you take a course in Scientology, you pay the tuition for the end result of what you get out of the course.

Certain courses can cost as much as fifteen thousand dollars and might take you two years to do. There's also counseling. That can be expensive. One hundred or two hundred dollars an hour. You become a member of the International Association of Scientologists. And that membership entitles you to a 10 percent discount off of everything you get.

Dianetics deals mostly with psychosomatic illnesses, unwanted attitudes, emotions, pains, sensations. Specific things. And it handles those things completely. I am happy. I love life. I have a lot of fun. I still have some shit. My own past is no longer having an effect on me in the present. Whereas the present *can* have an effect on me. And that's the reason why I have to get more training.

I've had a lot of ex-girlfriends. My problem is I'm an idealist. I really want to be in love with a person. And I really believe it could be there, but I haven't had it yet. I was engaged one and a half times. My longest relationship is about two years. That's terrible, I know. I think it's because I get bored easily. The ones I dumped, I just feel they weren't the right ones for me, and the ones that dumped me, I feel *all* of them were the right ones for me. But still. I feel like I'm missing something, I really do.

When I'm in a relationship and I start looking at other women and I wonder what they're like in bed.

I love variety and I love the excitement of new things.

I hadn't been close to my parents until last year. I always perceived myself as having a quote-unquote unhappy childhood. I grew up holding a grudge. Recently, they gave me a box of old pictures, and I looked *happy* in those pictures. I didn't look as if I was wanting for love or wanting for toys or anything like that. I had such a warped perception of myself, an ego problem, or a self-esteem problem, that it was quite remarkable.

I mentioned it to my parents, but I don't think they're coming at it from the same point of view as I'm coming from.

I mean, for me to look back on these pictures and to see myself sitting in this little fire truck wagon with my helmet on and a big smile on my face. I grew up with this perception that the only major Hanukkah present I got was a pencil sharpener. I had a very, very warped memory of my childhood.

Now, two days don't go by where I'm not on the phone to them, asking my parents how they're doing. Unfortunately it comes in the midst of all this other crap. They've been very supportive of me and my attempts to extricate myself from my marriage.

I met my wife when she was selling Avon products to a friend of mine. We were both in similar positions, both coming off other relationships. It was more comfortable than romantic. Our difficulties were never amicable, but they certainly shouldn't have been this divisive.

One of the reasons I chose to leave the marriage was because my children were getting such a bad idea of what a relationship between two people was. I thought that by moving out my wife would love them more because she wouldn't be constantly arguing with me. I thought I would love them more because I wouldn't be in that environment.

My friends tell me how heroic I am that I'm able to do this. But I don't see myself as being very heroic. I'm trying to maintain some sense where I'm not falling apart. That's just survival. It didn't have to be this way. It could have just been two people growing apart and being adult about it.

I know that I'm growing. I know that I'm becoming more valuable to myself, more normal, more true to my own instincts. On the other hand, this growth has come at such a price. It's frightening. For a while I thought I'd have to spend a hundred dollars to rent a best friend. You know, go into therapy. I did try it for a while. I didn't feel like this guy was really my friend.

My father put it to me this way—*You've got to do everything to stop the bleeding.*

Nat Tobin

Nicole Volta Avery

I went to Tuskegee University, in Alabama, which is an all-black college. It was a powerful feeling to be educated in an environment where race was not an issue. I grew up in Long Island, in an upper-middle-class neighborhood. I was the only black from third to twelfth grade. Out of a class of maybe 450. *The black girl.* It created a huge desire to be the best at everything. The best singer, the best athlete, to be a cheerleader. I didn't even *want* to be a cheerleader, but I had to get on the team. To be in the band, to be in *everything.*

On Halloween, my friend came to high school dressed as Aunt Jemima, and she wore the costume all day. I didn't say anything. I remember people avoiding me. We ultimately met up in the cafeteria. She comes over to me, and she's got this Aunt Jemima pancake syrup bottle, and she's holding this bottle. And they took a picture of her and I. And I'm smiling in the photograph.

My mother told me, these might be your so-called friends, but they'll publish that photo. I had talked to my mother about it, and I assured her that they wouldn't publish it because they were my "friends." They *did* publish it in the yearbook.

I got in a lot of trouble with my family for that. My parents grew up in the segregated South. I've had positive role models and I've heard the stories and my father marched with Martin Luther King. Black people. That photo for my parents was a slap in the face. At any time in my history as a person, that was a time for me to stand up, and I missed it.

I ceased being social at that point. My idea was that white people cannot be trusted. I'd given them all these chances, and they know me, they know I'm from a good family, they know I'm a nice person. These were my friends. It was deep.

And that is the primary reason why I went to Tuskegee.

Life at twenty-five is a series of catharses for me. I'm awakening to all these different things. I had a real aversion when I first came up to Syracuse living by myself. I associated living alone with loneliness. Now I really like it. I like listening to myself. Thinking out my life plans and goals in my own personal space, where the only noise being made is the noise I'm making.

My boyfriend says I sit in my house and marinate. I just kind of soak it all in.

I grew up in Havana. We had money, but it wasn't ostentatious. My father was a race car driver. It's not like we were living in a palace and having servants. We were comfortable, though, and we used to travel a lot.

My father sort of had this entourage. I always thought he was really cool. I loved it. He would take me to all these parties. He took me to Paris and Nice and Miami.

I was an only child, so I didn't need or have access to other children. And when I played with them, I really wanted to get back to my father or mother. Because in essence they were so much more fun. And I also sort of liked being a voyeur at these parties and watching everyone. Other children really didn't do it for me, the idea of having "buddies" and that sort of thing.

When I was four, we were at the beach in Havana, and there was a man there who had invented the daiquiri. He came up and started making all these daiquiris. And I started drinking them. My father gave me a whole bunch, so I got totally ripped. My first memory of being drunk. The daiquiris. My father was a very social person.

I went to high school in Philadelphia. I studied architecture in the Beaux Arts. I graduated valedictorian, so I got a scholarship to go to school. And I went to Penn. It was a great place to be at the time, to study architecture. I went to Penn for eight years—it was like being in a country club. It was great. Undergraduate and graduate school.

For a long time I was interested in the practice of architecture. Now I'm teaching. I worked for fifteen years. I had a company called Studio 300. Every time I would move, we'd change the name of the studio and reprint everything. People would think it was crazy, but it was great. It was always a number, but it would change every two years. I did a lot of architecture, furniture, interiors. Believe it or not, I've done things from skyscrapers to people's closets. It runs down the entire gamut. Size doesn't matter. I like it all.

Osvaldo Valdes

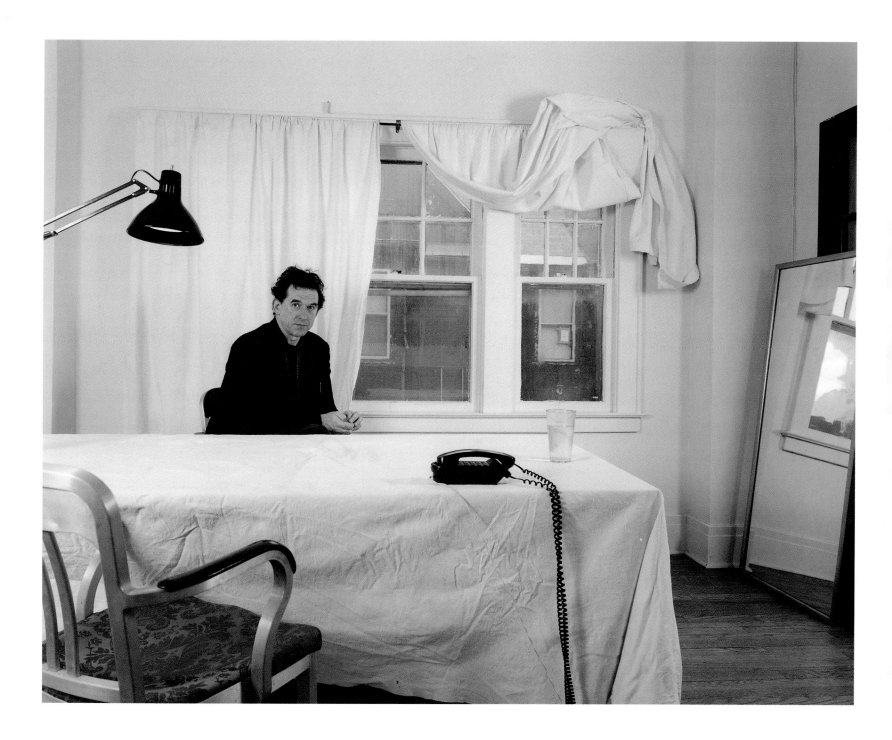

Rea Williams

I was divorced when my son was about six years old. My first husband was an alcoholic. My second husband died a good forty years ago. He was quite young, about thirty-five. He was a diabetic. And he smoked heavily, too. In those days, people smoked, you know. Then I remarried again. And I got a divorce from him. He was sort of a playboy and it didn't last.

Then there was another fellow. We sort of lived together. He died about eight years ago. I had seven years with him, and that was probably the most wonderful part of my life. We couldn't get married because he already was married and his wife wouldn't give him a divorce. At our ages, we figured, what's the use? With all the costs of fighting, it probably would have taken two or three years out of our fun life together. 'Cause we traveled all over the United States. We just had a great time. Spent a lot of time in Mexico. We loved to fish. Seven years of real happiness.

We had an RV, and we were ready to go up to Alaska. We had all the plans made. And he was working on the RV and he came in that evening and we were discussing our trip. And he said, "You know, I've got to take the RV up to get the muffler fixed." So he says, "I think I'll go to bed early," and I said, "Okay, I'll go to bed early, too." He had taken his shower and he crawled in bed and it was just *happiness*. He kissed me and we were on a high for this trip. And before I went to sleep, his hand came and hit me hard. And I kind of jumped out of bed and turned on the light and he was dead. He had a massive heart attack. That was a tremendous shock.

We were in love. Everything was great. So you have to think of all the nice things you had. But it was the most devastating moment of my life. It absolutely was.

I started drawing when I was real young. My dad was a barber and he had this barbershop and he used to put my charcoal drawings up in the barbershop. And there was this artist who was very well known at the time, and her husband was a doctor, and it was during the Depression and things were not that good. This was after I was out of high school. She offered to give me lessons and let me be her protégée if I'd come down and live at the house and kind of help with the housework and things. So I did that. That's when I started painting. I was the youngest member to ever get into the Women Painters of Washington at the time. And get into juried exhibitions. I think, had I not gotten married and things, I might have gone somewhere in art. But I got married and had my son and we had a totally different kind of life.

My daughter was born with cerebral palsy and deaf. It's a pretty mild case. She's not really spastic. We're not educated to take care of people with severe problems. A small percentage in the world should have children. And the rest of us should be aunts and uncles and just help out. Take them to the zoo or whatever. I was a terrible parent. I love my children, but I think having children is the most overestimated experience that you can have. I have two children in their forties now who still have problems. They're endless. We tend to blame ourselves if the children aren't perfect. I wouldn't do it again. And I know I wouldn't get married. They're both not for me. I was married thirty years.

I got divorced when I was fifty. Twenty-one years ago. It corresponded pretty much with the feminist revolution. That's when I was really born.

I met this young girl, Lynn, and had a very intense year photographing her. That's when I fell in love with her. It changed everything. It was a kind of an epiphany. She was eighteen and I was forty-two. She was my husband's student. We had her over for dinner one night and she asked me to photograph her. She didn't pose, but she was very natural. I made about twenty huge pictures and stuck them in her room as a surprise. And we became friends. I gave her a key to the studio. We had a date every Tuesday. We had the most outrageous year that I ever experienced. We would have picnics, champagne picnics on the floor.

I became a symbol to her of what she might become as a mature woman. Her family is very straight. She even had a coming out thing. Her opportunities were so much more exciting than mine, and so we shared this. It was not based on a sexual thing. It was almost biblical it was so intense. She was my daughter, she was me, she was what I could be. I was her mother, herself as an older woman. It was so complicated. We were not really lovers. Never were. But I did fall in love. And we maintain a relationship still.

Every year from the moment she took off, we have met somewhere in the world and taken at least a month or two. Just the two of us. Traveling or going somewhere or doing something. And we have done this for thirty years. I've had lots of relationships, and everyone is always annoyed with it and jealous of it. My kids, everyone finds it irritating. Except me and her. We have a most unusual relationship.

Living alone has interested me since I've been little. There's a different experience being by yourself than being with people. It's so different it's almost alarming. I think most people feel very threatened when they're alone. It could be that they just don't have enough to do to engage them on a level of fulfillment as a single unit.

Rita Hammond

84

I started working at the age of thirteen. I wanted to be independent. Make my own way. I worked in a grocery store. Then after that I started working in a factory. I worked in a dry-cleaning plant for a couple of years. From there I went to working in the hotel.

I started working in the linen room. Then I was a houseman. From there I went to operating the elevators. I operated the elevators for six years. That was a good chance for observation, and that was the beginning of getting to know most of the residential people who lived there in that hotel.

From that I got put on the front desk, and I did that for five or six years. We had elderly people. We had younger people who came from Connecticut and New Jersey to find their way after college. People who were starting out in the music field and acting. And today I have seen some of these same people on television in TV-made movies and commercials.

I have this way of making people feel comfortable. I'm definitely a very good listener. I was always told by a lot of people that I had a very winning smile and a very sunny disposition, and I think that sort of helped to draw these people to me. I was always there with a smile on my face and a cheerful "good morning" or "how-are-you" kind of thing. I think that was important. I was happy to be able to sit and talk with them and help them solve their problems. And it was kind of a learning experience also.

Then from that position I moved here. I started working in residential cleaning for a woman. A few of the steady customers, they said to me, Robert, why are you working for *her*? People started saying, You don't need her. When we recommend her service, we always say, Ask for Robert, because he's a terrific guy and he does a great job. So it didn't take me very long to sit down and say, Yeah, why not? I started my own business with three customers. And they called their friends, and that started a chain reaction. I do two houses a day. Believe it or not, I'd never have thought I'd enjoy what I'm doing. But I really like it.

I've been living alone for about ten years. I've had relationships where I was living with someone, but I think I'm happier living alone. I like the fact that I don't have to make any excuses for coming home late or not wanting to eat at a particular time.

When I was sick a couple weeks ago, there was no one here to fix anything for me. I had to do all that on my own. You learn to take care of yourself. It's awful when you're sick, but it's part of it.

Robert Harris

I'm part of the permanent infrastructure of musicians. Which means that I am a producer: I search out talent and I develop it and all of my stuff for the last year and a half has been signed to a major label.

I'm just on the cusp of being, like, one of the biggies.

The rock show is the fire that our primordial ancestors were around. The world is just piteously indifferent to anything that's not about moving the DNA along. What I do is Barney for teenagers. It's the soundtrack for teenage mating rituals, and that is its energy and that's where it helps move the DNA along and only insofar as it addresses that issue does it have an economic basis.

I like stars and hits. Stars first, hits second. Stars are magical to me. I know that I know how to make hits. I can write hits, I can produce them, I can record them. But a star I'm not. A star is magic. God makes them. We find them. You know. If we're lucky.

We all choose to look at reality through our own narrow lens. And mine's very sex/art driven. Marx said everything was economic. But I'm very sex/art. That's me.

I know I'm not crazy. I might get to a point where I feel I've really learned all I can from sanity, that's a pretty interesting thing to learn. See, I don't automatically demonize the experience of insanity. That's what I'm saying. It would be a choice. This is the unknowable. It's like knowing about death. You cannot know about being psychotic. By definition. You cannot have an awareness of it.

Roger Greenwalt

Sam McMillon

I started building furniture in 1959. I went to sixth-grade school. I built furniture a long time before I started painting it. I ain't been painting but for over ten years.

I started painting on some furniture, and I sold it to the lady I work for. She'd go get some chairs and stuff and I'd paint them. Take 'em back out there and she'd sell them for me. The trays you eat on, I paint mountains on them and she sell them. Everything is gonna be painted. They says I'm famous. They call me from everywhere night and day. I ain't rich. Be a long time before I get rich.

I love to paint. I love it. That more than anything. Painting is one thing that anything on your mind, you start painting, every bit of it leaves you, everything leaves you.

All my life, loved to work. Work hard. Loved to work better than go to school. I didn't want to go to school. I'd rather work for two days than go to school one day.

I chauffeured for twenty years. My man had tobacco warehouses in seven different states. I chauffeured President Johnson. I take him up to the airport. He was running with President Kennedy at that time.

Do you realize living alone, you can get up at three o'clock in the morning, you don't have nobody? You don't have to tip on your tip-toes. You can turn the TV on. Ain't no way in the world you'd be lonesome by yourself.

I'm a little person. A diastrophic dwarf. I never knew any other Little People until I was like twenty-four years old. I'd see other Little People on the street, or they'd try and talk to me, and I'd be like, I'm not like you. My family would always say, Don't be silly, you're fine. They would say stuff like, Oh, but you're much smarter than so and so. Or Well, you're prettier. But I saw that I was way littler and different.

When I finally went into therapy, I was able to bring out my feelings about the pain of being a Little Person, the jealousy I had. My therapist challenged me to find Little People of America and go to a meeting. I'm thinking, Fuck you, I really don't want to go to this. My feeling was that those people were all whiners, circus performers, or they were feeling sorry for themselves. Secretly, I felt sorry for myself, but I didn't want to admit it.

Two years later, this woman called me up, she was cool, she played the guitar. I thought she was incredibly depressing, but I liked her because she was artistic. She said, "Let's drive to the national Little People of America convention in St. Louis." So we did. There were a thousand Little People at that convention. I was expecting to see just a few people moping around. All the women were beautiful. And most of the men were really, really attractive. An incredible experience. The neat thing was the dances, because you could slow-dance with guys that were your same height.

The organization has become a meat market. Very competitive. I'd meet a guy from another part of the country, and I'd get real sexual with him right away. You don't get a chance to get to know him; they fly off five days later to some remote area of the country, and then you have these conversations on the phone until somebody can hop on a plane and visit. But then you're on your best behavior for those weekends.

I ended up joining SLAA which is Sex and Love Addicts Anonymous. It's really what changed my life. Because more so than a sex addict, I'm a love addict. I used to walk into a room and think, Okay, who can I get? That's how I would be. Almost like a mental slut. Even though I'm a Little Person, it made me different, and men liked that. Now I've set up bottom lines for myself—like no sex unless I'm in an intimate relationship. It's a twelve-step thing. Meeting other people who go through the same thing was phenomenal for me.

I really always wanted to live alone. When I was a kid, my favorite thing was to sit in boxes. You know, like this is *my* space. My little box. I love living alone because I tend to let people take advantage of me.

Tekki Lomnicki

Tom Maher

I came here to take care of my parents in 1979 because my father had had a stroke and my mother couldn't take care of him. He was bedridden for his last three years, then my mother needed my constant help. When he died, she was eighty-seven and she couldn't drive anymore. I didn't give it a second thought. There wasn't anything else I would have rather done at the time, other than take care of my parents.

My mother and I were never close emotionally. We had different personalities and interests. Sometimes they would coincide somewhat and we'd be all right. Like when my mother wanted to go pick strawberries, I'd go with her, and I got to like it. And blueberries. Things like that. She was from the South.

When my mother died in 1990, it was like the end of the world. This house, even though most of it was my own stuff by then, it seemed like an empty warehouse. The walls seemed strange and meaningless. It had lost its personality or whatever. Nobody else was here now. Just me. And what I was doing before had no relation to what I had to do now. I was like a lost boy. I went to a support group for bereavement, and the first thing I said up there was that I was a fifty-two-year-old orphan. And everybody knew what I meant because they were there for that same reason. Talking didn't help much. You're supposed to talk there, you know. It was terrible pain for at least a year. I just sat and stared. I had no idea what I was going to do. I was fifty-two years old. I had no real career. No real occupation. I had saved money ever since I had started working in 1968, and I had a few thousand dollars in the bank—twenty or thirty to be exact. I had saved for twenty-five years. So I wasn't panicky about my life financially.

When I was a kid I remember thinking that if my mother died, I didn't want to live.

She was ninety years old and still giving me lectures about things. So I didn't think it would bother me so much when she died because it was a natural thing. But it did. I was a total washout. I couldn't even think straight. It wasn't as though I was attached to my mother like some helpless kid. We were always like sparring partners in a way.

But everything added up to zero because my parents, by the time they died, all of the family had died. I was the last Maher in the whole entire clan of Mahers that had dominated a certain part of Kentucky for so long.

I'm the last Maher. I'm the end of the line.

Nineteen ninety-three was the Year of American Craft. By presidential procla-mation and joint resolution of Congress. So I got a letter that said that they were going to start a craft collection for the White House and they were going to pick thirty people's work for this and I was one of them.

I didn't know we were going to get invited to the White House. I had no idea. But there we were, we were kind of mingling around, and they had our stuff set up all over and we were talking. It was right at the holiday season.

Bill and Hillary came walking into the room. They had Marine guards all around. I was the first one in the receiving line. Hillary comes over and says, "Hello, I'm Hillary." I'm thinking, I knew *that*. Then we posed for the photograph. Then somebody comes up and says, "Bill wants you to see the Oval Office. We're going to take you on a little tour." So we went around, and they were showing us all these little rooms.

People were being very rude. Someone took Roosevelt's Nobel Peace Prize off the mantel, and starts looking at it. They were telling us not to touch anything. They were showing where the big meetings are held. The next day, I was waiting for the subway and I ran into someone else I knew; she had been in the next group, and she was telling me that she put her hand on Clinton's phone and her husband photographed her. I thought it was probably the nuclear button. She thought they were going to take her camera away. Clinton's college class ring was sitting on the desk, and someone picked it up, and said, "Hey, look, Clinton's ring!" They had to tell him to put it down and stop touching.

They had a great spread of food. They had a gingerbread White House. We weren't eating off of it, though. In another room, there was a boys' choir singing.

They had moved our coats, and when we walked outside to the Rose Garden, we wondered why they moved our coats. We found out very shortly. They gave us our coats, then we're outside walking along a walkway, and they showed us where the residential section is, then we walked through another door, and we're outside again, and the next thing we knew the doors closed behind us. And nobody was there, no more tour guide.

What a way to get rid of us!

I like living alone. I like doing what I want to do. I keep funny hours. When I was married, I was forced into going to family activities that I didn't want to go to, and parties, and having to get up at a certain time and do things.

Tom Muir

Tony Williams

I've always been a loner. I enjoy solitude and my own company. The human spirit fascinates me. Chemistry is just about putting together a puzzle, but the hardest puzzle of all is how the human functions. How does the human mind work? Why is it that if you eat shredded wheat this morning, your whole day can be affected by it? Because of sugar levels. Or somebody said two words to you yesterday that wiped you out for the whole day. What's that all about?

I read a pamphlet about the New Warriors which said it was an adventure weekend. I went to find out what it was all about. It has you look at things that may have affected you through life and get down to your feelings about them. Robert Bly says that one of the things men should feel is grief. As a culture, we stop ourselves from feeling, especially men, and as a result men get unfeeling toward women, I believe. I meet with my men's group every week. We sit around and talk, relive stuff. It's a safe place to share whatever has gone on in your day. I think I'm a lot better now. I wouldn't get angry before because the repercussions were always negative. There is a way to be angry and stay away from the repercussions. You can just be real clean, real clear.

The culture has shifted so quickly, and yet what's *ingrained* in men and women hasn't been able to keep up with it. The human capability, if you look around, has evolved incredibly quick, at an exponential rate. But the spiritual, in-depth basis for men and women to be distinct has not changed at that rate. So men are being asked to participate in a society with women where equality is becoming the chief form of having people share space. We're not equal. It doesn't mean that the male is the dominant race, the human is the dominant race. It just means that the expectations from us are different.

Men are terrified of men. Because the only place they've been known to have a connected, intimate relationship is with a woman. So many people of my age in the Western culture have grown up without close same-sex friends. I'm one of those, for sure. And for a number of the men I mix with that is a common story.

I'm from a village of sixty-three people in Wales. Nine miles to school, nine miles to the nearest town. I didn't really grow up around too many people. I'm the only one who left the village. All the kids I went to school with, they're still in the same pubs that they used to be. The last time I was home, there were four or five people in the pub who I went to primary and secondary school with, and *they knew me* and they didn't speak to me. Because I left, I'm different, and they disowned me. It's sad to have grown up in a place and have those connections as children and they just get hacked and broken down by age and growing up.

Vivian Grace

The reason my marriages didn't work is because I was very much involved in cocktails. And the second marriage was very brutal, there was a lot of abuse in it. A lot of physical abuse. When I left that marriage, I had two little girls, and we just *left*. My third marriage lasted the longest, and I had another daughter. I was raised to believe that you're supposed to be married and that you're supposed to have someone in your life.

I had my first drink when I was thirteen. By fifteen I drank to blackouts. By sixteen I was married. He was twenty-one when we got married, so he was my buyer. It was very sophisticated.

Drinking was so much a part of my life that I never even dreamed that I had problems *because* I drank, I thought I *drank* because I had problems. It was dinner and dysfunction at malfunction junction when I was growing up.

I wasn't there for my children. They would call me at a bar. I thought that was "being there" for them. They knew where to reach me. And it's really sad because my oldest daughter was in college at the end of my drinking, and she would come home to visit and she would come down to the bar to see Mom. My middle daughter fell in love and brought her boyfriend to meet Mom at the bar. We were close, but they had to come where I was, and they did that. My youngest daughter, who was sixteen when I got into recovery, said her goal in life was to get old enough to come to the bar and drink with me. It was really sad.

It was difficult to get in touch with my feelings. That was harder than putting down the bottle. I could tell you anything about me, all the things I had done, that I wasn't particularly proud of, and I had no secrets. I learned that we're as sick as our secrets. And I thought I wasn't that sick because I didn't have any secrets. But what I didn't realize until five years into recovery is my secrets were *feelings*. I could tell you what I'd done, but I couldn't tell you how I felt about it.

I don't believe in hopelessness. I had thirty years of bashing my head against the wall. I feel like I did all my suffering with the addiction prior to getting into recovery. So therefore I was given the gift of awareness.

When you first get into recovery, you really want to save the world. You want people to have what you've found.

I'm sixty-fucking-two. I'm a substance abuse counselor. I'm no longer a victim.

Afterword

LORIN ADOLPH (68–69) is a private chef in Chicago. He was born in 1963.

ELVIRA ALDERMAN (32–33) takes painting and sculpture classes at Syracuse University. She was born in 1907 in New York City. She worked as a model until she married in 1932.

ELAINE ARATA (30–31) is a freelance television writer. She wrote for *The Days and Nights of Molly Dodd*, among other television series, was a jazz dancer and choreographer, and is interested in glassblowing. She was born in 1960 and lives in Studio City, California.

NICOLE VOLTA AVERY (78–79) is a newspaper reporter for *the Syracuse Herald-Journal American*. She was born in 1969 and grew up in Westbury, Long Island.

ABBY BAYOUTH (2–3) was born in 1919. She is a retired interior designer.

LANCE BEAN (62–63) is a graduate student in industrial relations at Loyola University in Chicago, Illinois. He was born in 1970.

BARBARA BLANKS (12–13) is the director of community penalties and bunkum alternatives in North Carolina. She lives in Swannanoa, North Carolina. She directs a state program and is a state employee. She was born in 1938.

JOE BLAUSTEIN (54–55) is a painter living in Topanga Canyon, California. He was born in 1922.

CHRIS BRADLEY (24–25) is retired. He was born in 1907 and lives in Syracuse, New York.

AMY BRAKARSH (8–9) is a graduate student in interior design and architectural studies at Columbia College in Chicago. She was born in 1958 in New York.

JOAN COHEN (50–51) has her own landscaping business in Los Angeles.

JENNIFER CRISAFULLI (46–47) lives in New York City and works for *Rolling Stone* magazine. She was born in 1972 and grew up in Albany, New York.

LISA DANIELLE (64–65) is an artist living in Cornville, Arizona. She was born in an artists' colony in 1948 and grew up in Long Beach, California.

MARY-LOUISE DIGGS (70–71) is a volunteer at the Diggs Gallery in Winston-Salem, North Carolina. She was born in 1917.

ALBERT FANNING (6–7) is a freelance photographer in Syracuse, New York. He was born in 1946.

VIVIAN GRACE (100–101) is a substance abuse counselor in Asheville, North Carolina. She was born in 1933.

ROGER GREENWALT (88–89) produces musical acts, paints, and plays the guitar. He was born in 1960 and lives in New York City.

RITA HAMMOND (84–85) is a photographer in Cazenovia, New York. She teaches art history and photography at Cazenovia College and was born in 1924.

GORDON HARRINGTON (38–39) was a laborer in Camp Verde, Arizona. He worked for Chrysler at an assembly plant in Illinois for thirteen years. Several months after this interview he was seriously injured in a forklift accident. He has since married and is hoping to regain the use of his legs. He was born in 1949.

ROBERT HARRIS (86–87) was born in Brooklyn in 1940 and raised in the Bronx. He owns a residential cleaning service in Syracuse, New York.

JOAN HARRISON (52–53) is the vice president of miniseries at CBS. She was born in 1959 and lives in Los Angeles.

JUDD HOSTETLER (56–57) was born in 1930. Since 1990 he has been the coordinator and driver for Meals On Wheels in Brecksville, Ohio.

MICHAEL INGBAR (74–75) owns the Michael Ingbar Gallery of Architectural Art in New York City. He was born in 1945.

BRUCE LEDERMAN (16–17) owns and operates retirement residences. He lives in Chicago.

JUDE LEWIS (58–59) is an assistant professor in studio arts at Syracuse University. She was born in 1956 and has a dog named Connie.

TEKKI LOMNICKI (92–93) was born in 1956. She is a freelance copywriter, and writes and acts in one-person shows in Chicago.

SAM McMILLON (90–91) lives in Winston-Salem, North Carolina. He was born in 1925.

CAROLE MACKLER (20–21) was born in 1947 and raised on Long Island, New York. She owns her own tour company in Cornville, Arizona.

TOM MAHER (94–95) is a piano tuner and harpsichord builder in Syracuse, New York. He collects eighteenth-century-style figurines and ceramic flowers. He was born in 1938.

KIRBY MAJER (60–61) is a computer technician and consultant in Chicago, Illinois, who used to be a tour operator. He was born in 1947 in East Germany.

ANNE MEREDITH (10–11) is a screenwriter and lives in Beverly Hills, California. She wrote the screenplay for *Bastard Out of Carolina*.

ALAN METZGER (4–5) is a director for TV movies.

TOM MUIR (96–97) is a metalsmith and professor at Bowling Green State University. He was born in 1956 and lives in Perrysburg, Ohio.

ENID NEWFELD (34–35) was the executive assistant to the regional president of a distributor of computer printers. Now retired, she has three children and four grandsons. She was born in 1935.

HECTOR RODRIGUEZ (42–43) was born in Spain in 1972. He was raised in Puerto Rico, where his family still resides. He works for Christie's in New York City as an art handler.

EDDIE ROUSE (28–29) was born in 1952. He lives in Winston-Salem, North Carolina, and is an actor.

DAN SANTOW (26–27) is a project manager for Rand McNally in Chicago. He was born in 1960.

CHIKA SEKIGUCHI (22–23) released her debut CD, *Little Ship Head*, by Blue Marble Records, in 1997. She also owns her own graphic design company in Chicago. She was born in 1965.

HARVEY TERES (40–41) was born in 1949. He is an associate professor of English at Syracuse University.

NAT TOBIN (76–77) operates two art cinemas, in Syracuse and Manlius, New York—the Manlius Art Cinema and the Westcott Cinema. He was born in 1948.

JESSICA TUCK (48–49) is an actor in Los Angeles. She graduated from Yale and was born in 1963.

LISBETH UNGAR (66–67) lives in a high-rise apartment in Chicago. She was born in 1914 in Vienna, Austria.

OSVALDO VALDES (80–81) was born in Cuba. He is an architect and has been a professional chess player in New York City.

BYRON VREELAND (18–19) is an architect, a dentist, and a collector of Tiffany lamps. He lives in Los Angeles and was born in 1932.

BILL WALKER (14–15) is a television writer living in Los Angeles. He has written for *Roseanne, Frasier* (for which he won an Emmy in 1997), and *Cybill*. He was born in 1956 in Clinton, South Carolina.

MEL WHITE (72–73) is a director of African-American programs at a living history museum in Winston-Salem, North Carolina. Before this he was in banking. He has a graduate degree from banking school at Rutgers University and was born in 1941.

JEANNE WILLIAMS (44–45) graduated from Harvard Law School. She is an agent for ICM in Los Angeles. She was born in 1960.

REA WILLIAMS (82–83) lives in Leisure Village in Camarillo, California. She was born in 1912.

TONY WILLIAMS (98–99) was born in North Wales in 1964. He is a nuclear magnetic resonance spectroscopist working for Kodak in Rochester, New York. He looks at the nuclei of atoms and determines their molecular structure. He was educated in Liverpool and London, and did his postdoctoral work in Canada.

EVA WULKAN (36–37) is a retired medical technician. She was born in 1912 in Germany and lives in Chicago.